# Legal Reasoning

BORZOI BOOKS IN LAW AND AMERICAN SOCIETY

# Legal Reasoning

## Martin P. Golding
*Duke University*

ALFRED A. KNOPF        NEW YORK

This book was originally developed as part of an American Bar Association program on law and humanities with major funding from the National Endowment for the Humanities and additional support from the Exxon Education Foundation and Pew Memorial Trust. The ABA established this program to help foster improved understanding among undergraduates of the role of law in society through the creation of a series of volumes in law and humanities. The ABA selected a special advisory committee of scholars, lawyers, and jurists (Commission on Undergraduate Education in Law and the Humanities) to identify appropriate topics and select writers. This book is a revised version of the volume first published by the ABA. However, the writer, and not the American Bar Association, individual members and committees of the Commission, the National Endowment for the Humanities, Exxon Education Foundation, or Pew Memorial Trust, bears sole responsibility for the content, analysis, and conclusion contained herein.

THIS IS A BORZOI BOOK
PUBLISHED BY ALFRED A. KNOPF, INC.

First Edition

9 8 7 6 5 4 3 2 1

Copyright © 1984 by Alfred A. Knopf, Inc.

Library of Congress Cataloging in Publication Data
Golding, Martin P. (Martin Philip), 1930-
    Legal reasoning.

    (Borzoi books in law and American society)
    Bibliography: p.
    Includes index.
    1. Law—United States—Methodology. 2. Law—
Philosophy. 3. Judicial process—United States.
I. Title. II. Series.
KF380.G6  1983    340'.1    83-19919

        ISBN: 0-394-33191-5 (Paperbound)    0-394-33575-9 (Casebound)

Manufactured in the United States of America

# Preface

Every reader of this book is likely to have encountered excerpts from, and perhaps the whole of, judicial opinions in newspapers or in materials for courses in political science, history, or philosophy. Usually, and especially in the most important and interesting cases, these opinions will be elaborate *arguments* designed to support the decision or ruling of a judge on some *question of law;* for example, on the question: Does the United States Constitution permit the segregation by race of students in a public school? *Brown v. Board of Education,* 347 U.S. 483 (1954). Although the arguments in a judicial opinion are frequently quite long and complicated, an argument minimally consists of at least two statements, of which one (the premise) is claimed to be a *reason* for accepting the other (the conclusion). The term "argument" is sometimes also used to refer to just the reason or set of reasons for a particular statement, as when one challenges someone's assertion by asking him to give his arguments for it. Some arguments, however, are good arguments, and some are bad arguments; and one ought to be persuaded only by the good ones.

Traditionally, the study of arguments and the formulation of criteria for the evaluation of arguments has fallen within the domain of logic, but until fairly recently logicians had not given extended attention to legal arguments. This omission is currently being rectified, and new technical developments may provide interesting insights into the complexities and subtleties of legal reasoning. Nevertheless, the student who is in possession of only elementary branches of logic can go a rather long way in the understanding of legal arguments. Moreover, the study of elementary logic can be greatly enriched by the examination of judicial argumentation.

Logic, of course, is not the only academic or intellectual discipline concerned with argument or reasoning. Although the perspective of the logician is indispensable for studying judicial arguments, the perspective of other fields—particularly the normative fields of moral philosophy and political theory—are of equal importance. For these fields are concerned with the reasons that may be offered in order to justify a value judgment, decision, prescription for action, form of social organization, or system of government. As in moral and political arguments, judicial arguments frequently appeal to such considerations as justice, rights, fairness, welfare, and the common good. The analysis of legal reasoning, therefore, also requires that the insights of these fields be brought to bear on it. On the other hand, the subject matter of legal reasoning not only provides an endless source of interesting examples of normative arguments, which are grist for the mill of the ethical and political theorist, but its analysis may also shed considerable light on disputed issues in ethical and political theory.

This book of text, cases, and other materials is intended for use in courses in logic, ethics, political and legal philosophy, and other law-related undergraduate courses, primarily as a supplement to textbooks currently assigned. It is not intended as a book in ethics or logic or any subject other than legal reasoning, and it does not pretend to be a full-blown treatment of even that. Last but not least, it should be strongly emphasized that this book is not a text in the law. Many of the examples of judicial opinions used herein are outdated as statements of the law of any jurisdiction; but I believe all are excellent illustrations of significant facets of legal reasoning.

There are many issues in philosophy that are raised by topics treated in this book. Such issues include the questions: What is law? What purposes should law serve? What are the conditions for the validity of a law? These questions are not given any systematic treatment here, although the subjects and examples that are discussed provide suggestive avenues of approach to them. For systematic treatment, however, one will have to turn to other books, a few of which are mentioned in the bibliographic essay.

One important issue that does not receive systematic treatment is the relative roles of legislatures and courts in the development of the law. Legislatures have general lawmaking powers, while courts must wait for the presentation to them of a proper case before they can render decisions on questions of law. While both are constrained by the limitations set down by constitutions, courts are also constrained by statutes enacted by legislatures and (in the Anglo-American system) by precedents, the prior decisions of courts on questions of law. This division of role is reflected in the U.S. Constitution and state constitutions by the doctrine of "separation of powers," in which the executive, legislative, and judicial powers are distinguished. Although this important constitutional doctrine is not treated here, the reader will find topics that bear on it, particularly the "right of privacy" issue taken up in the *Roberson* and *Pavesich* cases, in Chapter 2, and the *Riggs* case, in the materials for that chapter.

Underlying the doctrine of separation of powers, however, is a more fundamental philosophical issue. Judges are supposed to decide cases "according to the law." They are supposed to be mere "mouthpieces of the law," in the words of the eighteenth-century French philosopher Baron de Montesquieu. (Montesquieu's book *Spirit of the Laws* had a significant influence on the framers of the Constitution.) Judges thus merely "declare" what the law is, according to Sir William Blackstone, the eighteenth-century English lawyer. (Blackstone's book *Commentaries on the Laws of England* was also influential in this country.) But to what extent can this "passive" conception of judicial decision making be maintained? Is it a realistic picture of what judges do? Do judges merely "find" the law when they decide questions of law, or do they sometimes also "make" law, and thereby exercise lawmaking power, as it were?

This fundamental issue is not explicitly discussed in this book, but there are discussions of topics that have a direct bearing on it; for example, the kinds of reasons judges give for regarding the premises of their arguments as true, the authoritative sources of the law, and good reason. The whole of Chapter 3 comes close to being a systematic treatment of this issue in the particular context of common (case) law development, but even there the discussion is more suggestive than definitive. The bibliographic essay contains references for readers who wish to pursue the matter more fully than it is treated in this book.

In order to enhance the usefulness of the opinions and materials that follow each chapter of text, each item is preceded by a brief introduction. Most items are also followed by a few questions, which can be used as a basis for class discussion or written assignments. The instructor may, of course, wish to introduce additional questions or topics for discussion or substitute other cases and materials. (I have tended to avoid cases that raise great constitutional issues.) Because of the length of Chapter 2, some instructors may find it advisable to turn to the materials for that chapter before starting on the section "Kinds of Reasons," although the materials will need to be done again when the text has been completed. Other variations are also possible. Many instructors will, in any event, find it necessary to supplement the examples of nonlegal arguments with additional examples and exercises.

I am grateful to the American Bar Association and its Commission on Undergraduate Education in Law and Humanities for their support of the development of these teaching materials. I extend my thanks to my students Marvin Belzer and John Hasnas, who assisted me in the early stages of my

work on this book, and to Allen Levine, who assisted me in the final stages.
The typing staff of the Duke Law School and, especially, Evelyn Holt-Fuller
are also deserving of my thanks. More than deserving of thanks is my wife,
Naomi. For many reasons, this book is dedicated to her.

MARTIN P. GOLDING

# Contents

# Citations

Throughout this book the reader will find references to cases. These references are written in the standard legal form of citation. These citations (commonly called "cites") include the name of the case, the volume number, the reporter (recorder), and the page where the case may be found. The year in which the case was decided is usually included in parentheses at the end of the citation.

Frequently, more than one citation is given for a case. In that event, the first cite is for the official state or federal recorder. The second is for the same case in the appropriate unofficial regional recorder. These secondary cites are called parallel citations.

Here are some examples from cases contained in this book:

*Lubitz v. Wells,* 19 Conn. Supp. 322, 113 A.2d 147 (1955)

The first cite, here, states that the case appears in volume 19 of the Connecticut Superior Court Reporter, starting on page 322. The second cite states that the case also appears in volume 113 of the Atlantic Recorder, Second Series, starting on page 147. The case was decided in 1955.

*MacPherson v. Buick Motor Co.,* N.Y. 382, 111 N.E. 1050 (1916)

In this example, the case is *MacPherson v. Buick Motor Co.* The first cite is to volume 217 of the New York Court of Appeals Reporter, page 382. The second cite is to volume 111 of the Northeast Reporter, page 1050. The case was decided in 1916.

Questions about citations and the specific abbreviations they use may be answered by referring to the standard guide, *A Uniform System of Citation.* It is published and distributed by the Harvard Law Review Association, Cambridge, Massachusetts 02138. The pamphlet may be found in any law library.

# Legal Reasoning

# I

# *The Study of Legal Reasoning*

The expression "legal reasoning" is used in a broad and a narrow sense. In the broad sense, it refers to the psychological processes undergone by judges in reaching decisions in the cases that are before them. These processes are comprised of ideas, beliefs, conjectures, hunches, feelings, and emotions. Loosely speaking, a judge's reasoning is what passes through his mind in the course of arriving at a decision, though in fact he may be barely conscious, or even not conscious at all, of many components of the process. In the broad sense, an occurrence of legal reasoning is part of the biography of some particular judge.

This book is about legal reasoning in the narrow sense, with particular focus on judges' decisions on questions of law. In the narrow sense of the term, "legal reasoning" refers to the arguments that judges give, frequently in written form, in support of the decisions they render. These arguments consist of the reasons for the decisions, and these reasons are intended as *justifications* for the decisions. Much of what passes through a judge's mind in reasoning, in the broad sense, about the case before him will not find its way into his argument. In offering their reasons, judges are attempting to justify their decisions to the interested public, which includes the parties to the case, other people who may be immediately affected by the decision, the legal profession, and the community at large.

A study of legal reasoning in the broad sense would be a study of judicial psychology and biography, which is important and interesting in its own right. The study of legal reasoning in the narrow sense is an inquiry into the "logic" of judicial decision making. It concerns the kinds of arguments judges give, the relationship between the reasons and the decisions, and the adequacy of these reasons as support for the decisions.

It is sometimes said that judges do not always reveal the real reasons for their decisions, and that the reasons they do present are no more than *rationalizations* for the results they reach.[1] This claim presumably is intended to suggest that in order to explain why a case is decided in a certain way, it is necessary to take into account factors that lie outside the explicitly given reasons. However, even if the claim is true, it in no way undermines the significance of an inquiry into the nature and logical force of judicial reasoning. A discussion of three points will reinforce this statement: discovery and justification in science and law, explanatory and justifying reasons, and reasoned decisions.

## Discovery and Justification in Science and Law

The process of scientific discovery often involves hunches, intuitions, and flashes of insight. These may be inspired by anything ranging from a scientist's religious beliefs to prior scientific knowledge to the stimulation of a drug. No history of scientific discovery would be complete if these factors were left out. However, what characterizes the process as *science* is not the hunch or its source but rather the attempt to subject the hunch, formulated as a hypothesis, to verification by carefully controlled experiment. The fact that the collection of evidence comes after the formulation of the hypothesis does not impugn the validity of the experiment. On completion of the experiment, the investigator can express the hypothesis as a *conclusion* inferred from the confirming data. It is obvious that the initial flash of insight, though undeniably important in the process of discovery, offers no grounds for accepting the hypothesis as true or probable. A history of science that ignored the reasoning by which results are established—the process of justification—would also be woefully incomplete.

Judicial decision making is analogous to the situation just described. The result in a case may be suggested to a judge in a flash of insight, but its rightness or acceptability can be shown only by providing reasons for it. When the judge writes his opinion, the insight, which initiated the process of deliberation (legal reasoning in the broad sense), will appear as the conclusion of an argument. And the strength of the argument will determine the acceptability of the decision just as much as the strength of the scientist's argument determines the acceptability of his results. This is not to suggest that judges conduct controlled experiments or that their arguments verify their

[1] On this point, see the selection by Jerome Frank, and the criticism of Frank by Richard A. Wasserstrom, in the materials for this chapter.

decisions as true or probable in exactly the same sense in which scientists verify hypotheses by appeals to confirming data. Nevertheless, in some respects the judge's argument serves one function that experiments perform in science. A judge may come to realize that an opinion "won't write"—that is, a defensible argument cannot be found for the result initially arrived at—so that he is led to decide the case differently.

The claim that a judge's explicitly given reasons are no more than rationalizations for a decision rests, in part, on a conflation of the process of discovery and the process of justification. It is true that judicial decision making is affected by the life history of the judge as well as by many other factors—after all, a case arises in a given social context and thereby acquires its specific social meaning—but one should not conclude from this that the explicit reasons have only a psychological or incidental interest. In attempting to understand what judges do, one can no more ignore the arguments they give than one can, in attempting to understand what scientists do, ignore the arguments scientists give.

At any rate, the claim is, at best, only a partial truth. It may rest on the correct observation that judges frequently do not explicitly state *all* the reasons (premises) on which decisions are grounded, as a logical analysis of judicial opinions shows. But this is no more a fault of judges than it is of everyone else, including scientists. Nevertheless, it is a point of great importance. In order to assess the force of a judge's argument it may be necessary to reconstruct it and bring out its tacit assumptions. Some of these assumptions, of course, will have been too trivial for the judge to mention; but others may prove to be quite substantial and debatable, yet the judge may not have been aware of them. It therefore is not surprising that someone should conclude that the explicitly given reasons are mere rationalizations. On the other hand, it is certainly false that the reasons judges give are never sincerely meant, or that judges are never persuaded by their own arguments. The objectivity and impartiality that are supposed to characterize the judicial process are features that derive in part from the logical requirements that control the process of justification.

## Explanatory and Justifying Reasons

Sometimes one wishes to explain why a certain event has occurred or why a certain general state of affairs exists. In these cases one seeks the causal conditions for the event or circumstance, and it is natural to call these conditions the reason (or reasons) for its occurrence. However, reasons of this sort, explanatory reasons, are not the only kind of reason. One also seeks the reasons for asserting a given judgment or statement to be true or correct. In this case one wants to know what the justifying reasons are. Because of the ambiguity of the expression "a reason for," it is easy to be misled into thinking that one kind of reason can be substituted for the other. Each type serves a function, has a use, that cannot be provided by the other.

It will be useful to illustrate this distinction, giving emphasis to the idea of justifying reasons, by an extended nonlegal—but lawlike—example. This example will also provide us with a few concepts necessary for subsequent discussions.

Suppose a professor assigns a term paper to his class. One member of the class has been particularly obstreperous during the semester, and the professor now has a perfect opportunity to "get back" at the student. The paper is given a failing grade, but it is returned with a long list of criticisms: poor organization, false statements, unsupported conclusions, and so forth. The student complains that the grade was motivated by the professor's desire for revenge; the professor counters by referring to his specific criticisms. What is the "real" reason for the failing grade in these circumstances?

The search for the "real" reason may be a search for a nonexistent quarry, and it might be useful, instead, to ask questions of the following sort: Was the professor so antagonistic toward the student that he would have given the paper a failing grade no matter what the student's performance on it was? Or, more weakly, would the paper have received such a low grade if the professor had not also felt antagonistic? In asking such questions, one is seeking to *explain* the assignment of the grade in much the same way as when one seeks to explain the occurrence of an event such as the collapse of a bridge—except that in a case such as this one, account is taken of psychological factors (purposes, motives, attitudes, etc.). One is looking for a causal explanation for a particular event. (Causal explanations, of course, are not confined to explaining particular occurrences. One also seeks causal explanations of types of circumstances or conditions, e.g., why rhododendron leaves curl up in cold weather.) If either of the above questions is answered affirmatively, one may want to say that the reason for the failing grade was the desire to get back at the student. Here, the term "reason" means "explanation."

Explanations of this sort, in terms of the socioeconomic status of the judge, racial bias, and so on, have been offered to explain specific judicial decisions and trends of decisions.[2] These explanations sometimes take into

---

[2] This issue is discussed in the materials for this chapter, in the selections from Harold Laski and Roscoe Pound, who refer to the case of *Priestley v. Fowler,* which is also included in the materials.

account the explicit reasons given for decisions, by construing such reasons as expressive of beliefs or values that have a psychological effect on the judge's action. The life history of the judge is relevant here. The Civil War experience of Justice Oliver Wendell Holmes, for instance, is claimed to have influenced his basic attitudes, which in turn are used to explain some of his decisions. More interestingly perhaps, these explanations also take into account factors that lie outside the explicitly given reasons or personal history. Every case arises in a specific political and social context, and is colored by that context. Economic and technological changes give rise to cases that would not have been presented in earlier periods. The full explanation of a decision or trend of decisions, therefore, may have to include the social context of the case. But no explanation of this sort will indicate whether a decision is correct or acceptable.

Let us return to the case of the failing term paper. Suppose that the student brings his complaint before an academic review committee, which has the power to overturn a grade that has been unfairly assigned. This committee will be interested in eliciting the facts surrounding the complaint: the student's behavior in class and the professor's attitude toward him. But it will primarily concern itself with whether the grade was deserved. The issue is not how the occurrence of a particular event is to be explained, but rather, whether a certain judgment or evaluation ("This is a failing term paper") is justified. The professor may acknowledge his antagonistic feelings, but he hardly will give them as a reason for the grade; and the committee will hardly consider them as justifying the grade. The committee members might, in fact, sympathize with the student; they might come to believe that the student's behavior was provoked by untoward conduct by the professor. But the main question before the committee is whether the criticisms of the paper are sufficient to justify the grade, that is, whether they are good reasons for it. A reason, in this regard, is a *justifying reason,* and it stands in contrast to the explanatory sort of reason ("The bridge collapsed because of the pressure of the flood waters") previously discussed. It is unlikely that the committee will try to explain the grade assignment unless it concludes first that the criticisms of the paper are inadequate to justify a failing grade.

One way to understand the situation just described is to think of the grade on the term paper as the conclusion of an argument, with the criticisms serving as reasons or premises for it. In order to do this, one has to express these elements in the form of propositions or statements, as follows:

(i)     This paper is poorly organized.
(ii)    This paper contains false statements.
(iii)   This paper has unsupported conclusions.
(iv)    Therefore, this is a failing paper.

This argument can be said to formulate the professor's reasoning, in the narrow sense mentioned earlier, in arriving at the grade. All reasoning, in this sense, can be characterized as the attempt to establish the truth, or correctness, or likelihood, or plausibility, or acceptability (the appropriate term is determined by the context) of some statement (the conclusion) by tendering another statement or set of statements (the premise or premises), which is alleged to provide support for it.

The academic review committee has the task of assessing the cogency of this argument. It will ask the following questions: (1) Are the premises (i), (ii), and (iii) true? (2) Are the characteristics referred to (poor organization, etc.) grade-relevant characteristics? (3) Are there any other grade-relevant characteristics that should be taken into account here? (Suppose, for instance, the paper contains a number of brilliant observations.) (4) If there are, do these other characteristics outweigh the ones referred to in the premises? The committee should attempt to answer these questions as impartially as it can, in accordance with its understanding of the standards that prevail in the teaching profession. Depending on how these questions are answered, the committee will either accept or reject the conclusion that the paper merits a failing grade. The cogency of the professor's argument, therefore, is objectively, if not mechanically, assessable in a manner that is independent of whether or not the explicit criticisms were only rationalizations for a decision that he reached on other grounds. The cogency of many judicial arguments can be assessed in a similar fashion.

## Reasoned Decisions

Most people who are at the losing end of a case are not very happy with the outcome. The stakes at issue may have been high: years behind bars in a criminal case, a great deal of money in a civil case. Even if the issue in a civil case seems trivial to an outsider, it must have been important enough to the parties for them to have pursued their dispute in a court of law. So the loser may complain about the result. But is he *entitled* to complain? One of the important functions of the reasoned decision—a decision for which the judge or official articulates the (justifying) reasons—is to enable this question to be answered.

Since the concern in this book is primarily with how judges justify their rulings on questions of law, it is important to note that the average case before a court deals with disputes over questions of fact (e.g., Was the traffic light red or green when Smith's car passed through?) rather than with questions of law. If a court (the judge or jury) gives wrong answers to the main questions of fact in a case, the outcome will be legally unjust. It is essential, therefore, that courts should employ fair and rational procedures for arriving at the correct (or the humanly best) answers to these factual questions. This means that the parties should be given adequate opportunity to prepare their cases, that they should be given a fair opportunity to present their evidence, and that each party should be given a fair chance to respond to the evidence presented by the opposing side.

In the American legal system the "adversary" method of truth discovery is generally used, in which the parties (or more usually their lawyers) take an active role in litigating the questions of fact before the court, rather than a method in which the judge conducts an independent inquiry into the factual issues surrounding the dispute. It is believed that the adversary method promotes the cause of legal justice, because each party will bring to the attention of the court all the material it holds to be favorable to its side of the dispute, and no relevant evidence will be ignored. The truth, it is believed, will emerge out of the clash between the parties. It is also thought that in a criminal case, the rights of the accused are best protected under the adversarial system. Whether or not all this happens depends, of course, on a number of factors, for example, the competence of the lawyers. If one may assume that these truth-discovery procedures are fair and rational (the rationality of the adversary method has been attacked on the ground that judges and juries are not necessarily the most competent weighers of evidence), losing litigants are likely to feel that they got a "fair shake" and will not complain about the outcome. The losers should feel, at least, that the outcome was reasonable, if not right. But even if they are dissatisfied with the outcome, independent observers will not think them entitled to complain. And this is extremely important, because society has a strong interest in maintaining the integrity of the processes by which citizens are deprived of their liberty or their property.

In the average case, then, it is issues of fact that are in dispute. But what these issues of fact are depends on the relevant law. (The color of the traffic light is of concern only because there is a law prohibiting going through red lights.) In the average case, the rules of law will be clear and not in dispute. But in some cases—usually the most interesting cases, philosophically—the parties are in agreement on the facts but disagree over what the law as applied to those facts is. And when a judge does have to rule on what the law is, it is also extremely important that rational procedures should be followed. The potential loser, and society at large too, has a strong interest that decisions on questions of law should not be made arbitrarily. (The adversary method also plays an important role when questions of law are at issue. Each party will bring to the court's attention all the statutes, precedents, and legal principles favorable to its position, so that no relevant consideration will be ignored.)

Strictly speaking, however, there is no sure-fire procedure for discovering correct answers to questions of law, any more than there is a sure-fire procedure for making significant discoveries in science. When faced with difficult questions of what the law is, judges naturally will go through a reasoning process of search and reflection—legal reasoning in the broad sense. But in order to ensure that their decisions are not arbitrary, they will have to articulate the reasons for their decisions—that is, justify them by giving arguments for them. Of course, it would be unfortunate if a judge's argument was a mere rationalization and if the judge did not sincerely hold the reasons he explicitly gives. But in an important respect this fact, whenever it is a fact, is irrelevant to the justifiability of the decision. The justifiability of the decision depends on how well the decision is reasoned.

It should be plain that judges do not engage in reason giving or opinion writing merely as an intellectual performance. (In most jurisdictions in the United States, written opinions are neither required nor reported at the trial court level. But written opinions usually are provided when important questions of law are at issue and especially at the appellate court level, which is concerned almost exclusively with questions of law.) A judicial justification is not simply an argument that exists abstractly in some conceptual realm. A justification is offered in order to *justify to* someone the decision or conclusion; a justification is directed to an audience. Perhaps the first person to whom the justification is directed is the losing litigant; and to this may be added all other people whose interests might be adversely affected by the result. These persons need to be assured that the administration of the law is not just a bald exercise of coercion, that it is not the might of the judge (the power of enforcement) that makes the decision right. Reasoned decisions, therefore, can be viewed as attempts at *rational persuasion*; and by means of such decisions, losing parties may be brought to accept the result as a legitimate exercise of authority. If this acceptance is achieved, the cause of social peace is also promoted, since every case has a loser. The system of administering justice through the courts is not likely to survive for very long if half the people whose disputes are resolved are convinced that judges arbitrarily decide questions of law.

In making an effort at rational persuasion, judges show respect for their audience by addressing its members as rational individuals, and it is clear that such individuals are not going to be persuaded by just *any* reasons a judge might give. The reasons will have to be regarded by them as *good reasons* for the decision. What this means is something that we shall be concerned with in the later chapters of this book. Provisionally, however, let it be said that a good reason (a premise in the judge's argument) is (1) a statement that is, in some sense, true or acceptable and (2) a statement that is relevant to the decision (conclusion)—two points that played a role in the term paper example discussed earlier. If one regards the judge's reasons as good reasons for the decision and can find no countervailing considerations, then one ought to accept the judge's decision. Of course, the losing litigants will not be very happy with the outcome; but unless they can persuade one that the judge's reasons are not good or that there are countervailing considerations, one will not think them entitled to their complaint. In any case, even if the losers are not persuaded by the judge's argument, they may still be persuaded enough by it to acknowledge that the judge's ruling was one that a reasonable person could arrive at, and so, that the decision was not made arbitrarily.

The fact that rational individuals are not persuaded by just any reasons that a judge could conceivably give has an important consequence: the reasons have to be more than an expression of the judge's personal predilections. These reasons, therefore, operate as *controls* on the process of deliberation. Since judges are aware that they will have to supply a public justification of their rulings, any hunch, flash of insight, or "gut feeling" they initially had about a case before the court will be tested against the kinds of reasons that are likely to be appealing to their audience. The deliberation process, legal reasoning in the broad sense, need not be an entirely arational or irrational affair. Second, the judges' reasons will have an *objective* status in a significant degree. Ideally, a judge's reasons should be reasons that the losing litigant will recognize as good reasons; but in any event the judge will want his or her reasons to be reasons that independent observers, especially other judges and lawyers, will find acceptable. Of course, it is not necessarily the case that all independent observers will agree with the judge—as the history of American courts shows. Still, the fact that judges have to justify their decisions to an audience of rational persons is a highly significant feature of judicial argumentation.

Reasoned decisions serve other functions besides that of trying to convince people that judges do not act arbitrarily. A judge's decision in a case is also meant to supply *guidance* to other individuals on what the law is and on how their cases are likely to be decided should they end up in court, so that those individuals can adjust their conduct accordingly. But a decision can serve this function only if reasons are given, otherwise all one has is an unconnected series of raw facts. One has to know which facts are legally significant—which is what the reasons indicate. (The fact that the man who went through the red light was named Smith is not legally significant, but the fact that he was on his way to a hospital may be crucial.) Second, appellate courts are supposed to supply legal guidance to lower courts, and because of considerations similar to those just mentioned, their decisions will not be very helpful unless they lay out the reasons for their rulings. And third, in the American system many decisions are justified by reference to precedent—the decisions made in prior cases. Again, it is only because explicit reasons were given for these earlier decisions that they are of any use for later cases. Plainly, many of the functions that courts serve require reasoned decisions.

Enough has been said to dispose of the view that the study of legal reasoning, the explicit arguments judges give, is of no importance and also, perhaps, of the claim that judges' reasons are mere rationalizations. This chapter closes with a final comment on the idea that judges are not sincere about the reasons they give for their decisions. If this criticism is to have any force in undercutting the study of judicial reasoning, a clearer idea of its meaning is needed.

To say that a judge is not sincere is to say that he is not prepared to apply the same reasons that he gives in one case to the deciding of another case which involves a similar set of facts or which raises a similar legal issue; that is, that the judge feels no demand for *consistency* in the way he decides cases. The fact is that judges, since they may have to give a public justification of their rulings, are very much concerned with consistency. Plainly, a judge's decisions would offer no guidance for the future conduct of individuals if they could not count on judges to be consistent to a large extent. As to legal argument, judges frequently do test their reasoning by considering how they would decide other similar cases, actual and hypothetical.

We shall see later that the notion of case-to-case consistency plays an important role in judicial reasoning. Still, judges' arguments are not always well articulated, and judges sometimes do fall into inconsistency, which in itself does not signify that judges are insincere. This is not to imply, though, that judges are never insincere or that judges are always honest and aboveboard in the way they make and defend their rulings.

A few paragraphs earlier it was pointed out that a rational individual is not going to be persuaded by just any reasons a judge may give. Two provisional criteria of good reasons were mentioned: truth (or acceptability) and relevance. Before proceeding to the topic of good reasons, however, some detailed consideration must be given to the types of arguments judges put forward.

## MATERIALS

*Jerome Frank,*
*The Judging Process (1930)* *

=================

*Jerome Frank (1889-1957) served as an official in three of President Franklin D.*
*Roosevelt's New Deal agencies and was a judge of the U.S. Court of Appeals for the*
*Second Circuit from 1941 to 1957. He is best known as a forceful proponent of the*
*"legal realist" movement, which blossomed in the 1930s. Basically, legal realists*
*believed that less attention should be paid to "book law" and more to the way law ac-*
*tually works. Frank was interested in psychoanalysis and broke new ground by apply-*
*ing a Freudian perspective to the law in his most famous work,* Law and the Modern
Mind *(1930). In the following excerpt from that book, Frank argues that judges are*
*just like all other people, in that nonrational forces play a major part in their decision-*
*making processes.*

### The Process of Rationalization

The ideas and beliefs of all of us may be roughly classified as of two
kinds: those that are based primarily on direct observation of objective data
and those that are entirely or almost entirely a product of subjective factors—desires and aims which push and pull us about without regard to the
objective situation.

These beliefs of the second kind are usually emotionally toned to a high
degree. We are usually more or less unaware of their existence although
they have marked effects upon our thinking. For convenience we may refer
to any such belief as a "bias."

I am, let us say, an ardent Republican. The Republican party is in office
and puts through a new high protective tariff. An election campaign ensues
in which the merits of this tariff are in controversy. I advance many reasons
in support of the Republican tariff. Now, I have not carefully investigated
the problem and my arguments have little reference to the actual facts. Yet
in a short time I convince myself that the Democrats are unreasonably opposing my party's position. I am sure that my views are the result of my
"reasons" whereas the real determinant of my views is my political "bias"
and my "reasons" are more or less illusory and after the fact. But I would
most reluctantly make such an admission. I have a stubborn pride in my

---

* Jerome Frank, *Law and the Modern Mind* (Garden City, N.Y.: Doubleday, Anchor Books,
1963), pp. 31-33, 108-115. Reprinted from Jerome Frank, *Law and the Modern Mind*, originally published by Brentano's Inc. in 1930. Copyright by Brentano's Inc. Copyright 1930, 1933,
1949 by Coward McCann. Copyright renewed in 1958 by Florence K. Frank. These excerpts
are taken from the Anchor Books edition, published in 1963 by arrangement with Barbara Frank
Kristein, and are here printed with the permission of Marvin Kristein, executor of the estate of
Barbara Frank Kristein. All rights reserved.

rationality and cannot easily let myself know that my thoughts are responsive to non-rational aims and impulses.

Such a political bias is relatively superficial. Our most compelling biases have deeper roots and are far better concealed from consciousness. They often grow out of childish aims which are not relevant to our adult status. To admit their existence would be difficult and painful. Most of us are unwilling—and for the most part unable—to concede to what an extent we are controlled by such biases. We cherish the notion that we are grown-up and rational, that we know why we think and act as we do, that our thoughts and deeds have an objective reference, that our beliefs are not biases but are of the other kind—the result of direct observation of objective data. We are able thus to delude ourselves by giving "reasons" for our attitudes. When challenged by ourselves or others to justify our positions or our conduct, we manufacture *ex post facto* a host of "principles" which we induce ourselves to believe are conclusions reasoned out by logical processes from actual facts in the actual world. So we persuade ourselves that our lives are governed by Reason.

This practice of making ourselves appear, to ourselves and others, more rational than we are, has been termed "rationalization."

Rationalization not only conceals the real foundations of our biased beliefs but also enables us to maintain, side by side as it were, beliefs which are inherently incompatible. For many of our biased beliefs are contradicted by other beliefs which are related more directly to clear reasoning from real knowledge of what is going on in the outside world . . . . The incompatible beliefs or ideas are allowed to meet, but only by means of "a bridge of rationalizations." In this manner the logical significance of each of the antagonistic beliefs or ideas is so distorted that the conflict between them is concealed.

## The Judging Process and the Judge's Personality

As the word indicates, the judge in reaching a decision is making a judgment. And if we would understand what goes into the creating of that judgment, we must observe how ordinary men dealing with ordinary affairs arrive at their judgments.

The process of judging, so the psychologists tell us, seldom begins with a premise from which a conclusion is subsequently worked out. Judging begins rather the other way around—with a conclusion more or less vaguely formed; a man ordinarily starts with such a conclusion and afterwards tries to find premises which will substantiate it. If he cannot, to his satisfaction, find proper arguments to link up his conclusion with premises which he finds acceptable, he will, unless he is arbitrary or mad, reject the conclusion and seek another.

In the case of the lawyer who is to present a case to a court, the dominance in his thinking of the conclusion over the premises is moderately obvious. He is a partisan working on behalf of his client. The conclusion is, therefore, not a matter of choice except within narrow limits. He must, that is if he is to be successful, begin with a conclusion which will insure his client's winning the lawsuit. He then assembles the facts in such a fashion that he can work back from this result he desires to some major premise which he thinks the court will be willing to accept. The precedents, rules, principles and standards to which he will call the courts attention constitute this premise.

While "the dominance of the conclusion" in the case of the lawyer is clear, it is less so in the case of the judge. For the respectable and traditional descriptions of the judicial judging process admit no such backward-working explanation. In theory, the judge begins with some rule or principle of law as his premise, applies this premise to the facts, and thus arrives at his decision.

Now, since the judge is a human being and since no human being in his normal thinking processes arrives at decisions (except in dealing with a limited number of simple situations) by the route of any such syllogistic reasoning, it is fair to assume that the judge, merely by putting on the judicial ermine, will not acquire so artificial a method of reasoning. Judicial judgments, like other judgments, doubtless, in most cases, are worked out backward from conclusions tentatively formulated.

As Jastrow says, "In spite of the fact that the answer in the book happens to be wrong, a considerable portion of the class succeeds in reaching it. . . . The young mathematician will manage to obtain the answer which the book requires, even at the cost of a resort to very unmathematical processes." Courts, in their reasoning, are often singularly like Jastrow's young mathematician. Professor Tulin has made a study which prettily illustrates that fact. While driving at a reckless rate of speed, a man runs over another, causing severe injuries. The driver of the car is drunk at the time. He is indicted for the statutory crime of "assault with intent to kill." The question arises whether his act constitutes that crime or merely the lesser statutory crime of "reckless driving." The courts of several states have held one way, and the courts of several other states have held the other.

The first group maintains that a conviction for assault with intent to kill cannot be sustained in the absence of proof of an actual purpose to inflict death. In the second group of states the courts have said that it was sufficient to constitute such a crime if there was a reckless disregard of the lives of others, such recklessness being said to be the equivalent of actual intent.

With what, then, appears to be the same facts before them, these two groups of courts seem to have sharply divided in their reasoning and in the conclusions at which they have arrived. But upon closer examination it has been revealed by Tulin that, in actual effect, the results arrived at in all these states have been more or less the same. In Georgia, which may be taken as representative of the second group of states, the penalty provided by the statute for reckless driving is far less than that provided, for instance, in Iowa, which is in the first group of states. If, then, a man is indicted in Georgia for reckless driving while drunk, the courts can impose on him only a mild penalty; whereas in Iowa the judge, under an identically worded indictment, can give a stiff sentence. In order to make it possible for the Georgia courts to give a reckless driver virtually the same punishment for the offense as can be given by an Iowa judge, it is necessary in Georgia to construe the statutory crime of assault with intent to kill so that it will include reckless driving while drunk; if, and only if, the Georgia court so construes the statute, can it impose the same penalty under the same facts as could the Iowa courts under the reckless driving statute. On the other hand, if the Iowa court were to construe the Iowa statute as the Georgia court construes the Georgia statute, the punishment of the reckless driver in Iowa would be too severe.

In other words, the courts in these cases began with the results they desired to accomplish: they wanted to give what they considered to be adequate punishment to drunken drivers. Their conclusions determined their reasoning.

But the conception that judges work back from conclusions to principles is so heretical that it seldom finds expression. Daily, judges, in connection with their decisions, deliver so-called opinions in which they purport to set forth the bases of their conclusions. Yet you will study these opinions in vain to discover anything remotely resembling a statement of the actual judging process. They are written in conformity with the time-honored theory. They picture the judge applying rules and principles to the facts, that is, taking some rule or principle (usually derived from opinions in earlier cases) as his major premise, employing the facts of the case as the minor premise, and then coming to his judgment by processes of pure reasoning.

Now and again some judge, more clear-witted and outspoken than his fellows, describes (when off the bench) his methods in more homely terms. Recently Judge Hutcheson essayed such an honest report of the judicial process. He tells us that after canvassing all the available material at his command and duly cogitating on it, he gives his imagination play,

and brooding over the cause, waits for the feeling, the hunch—that intuitive flash of understanding that makes the jump-spark connection between question and decision and at the point where the path is darkest for the judicial feet, sets its light along the way. . . . In feeling or "hunching" out his decisions, the judge acts not differently from but precisely as the lawyers do in working on their cases, with only this exception, that the lawyer, in having a predetermined destination in view—to win the lawsuit for his client—looks for and regards only those hunches which keep him in the path that he has chosen, while the judge, being merely on his way with a roving commission to find the just solution, will follow his hunch wherever it leads him. . . .

And Judge Hutcheson adds:

"I must premise that I speak now of the judgment or decision, the solution itself as opposed to the apologia for that decision; the decree, as opposed to the logo-machy, the effusion of the judge by which that decree is explained or ex-cused . . . . The judge really decides by feeling and not by judgment, by hun-ching and not by ratiocination, such ratiocination appearing only in the opinion. The vital motivating impulse for the decision is an intuitive sense of what is right or wrong in the particular case; and the astute judge, having so decided, enlists his every faculty and belabors his laggard mind, not only to justify that intuition to himself, but to make it pass muster with his critics. (Accordingly, he passes in review all of the rules, principles, legal categories, and concepts) which he may find useful, directly or by an analogy, so as to select from them those which in his opinion will justify his desired result."

We may accept this as an approximately correct description[1] of how all judges do their thinking. But see the consequences. If the law consists of the decisions of the judges and if those decisions are based on the judge's hun-ches, then the way in which the judge gets his hunches is the key to the judicial process. Whatever produces the judge's hunches makes the law.

What, then, are the hunch-producers? What are the stimuli which make a judge feel that he should try to justify one conclusion rather than another?

The rules and principles of law are one class of such stimuli.[2] But there

---

[1] Which confirms what was said above . . . about judicial "rationalizations." See Hutcheson, "The Judgment Intuitive: The Function of the 'Hunch' in Judicial Decisions," 14 Cornell Law Quarterly, 274.

A century ago a great American judge, Chancellor Kent, in a personal letter explained his method of arriving at a decision. He first made himself "master of the facts." Then (he wrote) "I saw where justice lay, and the moral sense decided the court half the time; I then sat down to search the authorities. . . . I might once in a while be embarrassed by a technical rule, but I almost always found principles suited to my view of the case. . . ."

[2] If Hutcheson were to be taken with complete literalness, it would seem that such legal rules, principles, and the like are merely for show, materials for window dressing, implements to aid in rationalization. They are that indeed. But although impatience with the orthodox excessive emphasis on the importance of such devices might incline one at times to deny such formula-tions any real value, it is necessary—and this even Hutcheson would surely admit—to concede them more importance. In part, they help the judge to check up on the propriety of the hun-ches. They also suggest hunches.

are many others, concealed or unrevealed, not frequently considered in discussions of the character or nature of law. To the infrequent extent that these other stimuli have been considered at all, they have been usually referred to as "the political, economic and moral prejudices" of the judge.[3] A moment's reflection would, indeed, induce any open-minded person to admit that factors of such character must be operating in the mind of the judge. But are not those categories—political, economic and moral biases—too gross, too crude, too wide? Since judges are not a distinct race and since their judging processes must be substantially of like kind with those of other men, an analysis of the way in which judges reach their conclusions will be aided by answering the question, What are the hidden factors in the inferences and opinions of ordinary men? The answer surely is that those factors are multitudinous and complicated, depending often on peculiarly individual traits of the persons whose inferences and opinions are to be explained. These uniquely individual factors often are more important causes of judgments than anything which could be described as political, economic, or moral biases.

In the first place, all other biases express themselves in connection with, and as modified by, these idiosyncratic biases. A man's political or economic prejudices are frequently cut across by his affection for or animosity to some particular individual or group, due to some unique experience he has had; or a racial antagonism which he entertains may be deflected in a particular case by a desire to be admired by someone who is devoid of such antagonism.

Second (and in the case of the judge more important), is the consideration that in learning the facts with reference to which one forms an opinion, and often long before the time when a hunch arises with reference to the situation as a whole, these more minute and distinctly personal biases are operating constantly. So the judge's sympathies and antipathies are likely to

---

[3] Most of the suggestions that law is a function of the undisclosed attitudes of judges stress the judges' "education," "race," "class," and "economic, political and social influences" which "make up a complex environment" of which the judges are not wholly aware but which affect their decisions by influencing their views of "public policy," or "social advantage" or their "economic and social philosophies" or "their notions of fair play or what is right and just."

It is to the economic determinists and to the members of the school of "sociological jurisprudence" that we owe much of the recognition of the influence of the economic and political background of judges on decisions. For this, much thanks. But their work has perhaps been done too well. Interested as were these writers in problems of labor law and "public policy" questions, they over-stressed a few of the multitude of unconscious factors and over-simplified the problem. . . .

be active with respect to the persons of the witness, the attorneys and the parties to the suit.  His own past may have created plus or minus reactions to women, or blonde women, or men with beards, or Southerners, or Italians, or Englishmen, or plumbers, or ministers, or college graduates, or Democrats. A certain twang or cough or gesture may start up memories painful or pleasant in the main.  Those memories of the judge, while he is listening to a witness with such a twang or cough or gesture, may affect the judge's initial hearing of, or subsequent recollection of, what the witness said, or the weight or credibility which the judge will attach to the witness's testimony.

## QUESTIONS

1. Frank contends that the conclusions judges wish to reach determine their reasoning. Can you give examples from everyday life that illustrate this contention?
2. Does identifying one's biases and prejudices help in overcoming them?
3. See footnote 2 of the selection. Is it compatible with the tenor of Frank's thesis? Or does he give back with one hand what he has taken away with the other?

## *Richard A. Wasserstrom,* <br> *Judicial Decision Making (1961)* *

*Richard A. Wasserstrom (1936-   ) was formerly dean of the College of Arts and Sciences at Tuskegee Institute and a professor of law and philosophy at the University of California (Los Angeles). He is now chairman of the philosophy board at the University of California (Santa Cruz). He has published many articles on racial discrimination and other contemporary moral issues. In this excerpt from a 1961 book,* The Judicial Decision, *Wasserstrom draws a distinction between the process of reaching a conclusion ("discovery") and the process of justifying the conclusion ("justification"). He uses this distinction to criticize Frank.*

Earlier it was observed that the question "What is the nature of the judicial decision process?" might be ambiguous, since it is not clear whether a descriptive or a prescriptive reply is being requested, nor whether this is a demand for a single monolithic response that must adequately describe all decisions, or only a request for an answer that can account for the most im-

* Reprinted from Richard A. Wasserstrom, *The Judicial Decision: Toward a Theory of Legal Justification* (Stanford, Calif.: Stanford University Press, 1961), pp. 25-31, with the permission of the publishers, Stanford University Press. ©1961 by the Board of Trustees of the Leland Stanford Junior University.

portant or significant ones. In the light of the foregoing discussion it is necessary to ask whether there may not be still a third kind of ambiguity contained within or implied by the question. For the phrase "judicial decision process" is, I submit, capable in itself of denoting two quite different procedures, neither of which has as yet been carefully isolated or described. And until this is done, intelligent inquiry into the nature of the judicial decision process cannot be effected, nor can the issue of the correctness of the deductive theory be resolved.

Placing the problem within the broader context of decision procedures in general, there are two quite distinctive procedures that might be followed before any particular decision is made or accepted. This is as true in science or ethics as it is in law. The way in which these two procedures operate can be indicated by reference to two types of questions that may be asked about any decision. One kind of question asks about the manner in which a decision or conclusion was reached; the other inquires whether a given decision or conclusion is justifiable. That is to say, a person who examines a decision process may want to know about the factors that led to or produced the conclusion; he may also be interested in the manner in which the conclusion was to be justified.

Consider the following three examples:

(1) I see a person helping a blind man across the street and I ask him why he aided the blind man. The person might reply: "I helped him because I thought he would give me a tip."

(2) A scientist who has discovered a vaccine which purportedly provides complete immunization against cancer informs the scientific community that he hit upon this particular chemical combination in the following manner. He wrote down 1,000 possible chemical combinations on separate pieces of paper, put them all into a big hat, and pulled out one of the pieces at random.

(3) Charles A. Beard reports that the drafters of the Constitution were members of the propertied class who desired to perpetuate many of their own class values within the framework of the new government.

Now, all three of these examples tell something about how a particular conclusion or decision was reached. None of these examples, it can be argued, answers the question of whether any one of these conclusions is in any sense a justified or justifiable conclusion.

In the first example it might be argued that the answer given is irrelevant to the question of whether the action of helping a blind man to cross a street (the decision or conclusion) is a morally desirable act. For both parties might agree that the expectation of a reward does not constitute a morally good reason for behaving in a specified manner.

The second example makes the point still clearer. The scientist has announced how he arrived at the conclusion that this chemical formula might immunize against cancer, but of course he has not answered the question of whether the vaccine will in fact immunize. How the scientist happened to select the formula is one question. Whether this formula is an effective vaccine, whether the conclusion can be empirically validated, is quite a different one. Furthermore, if *ex hypothesi* the vaccine were effective, it would certainly not be rejected because of the way in which the scientist selected it for testing.

In the same manner and for the same reasons, it may be observed that a knowledge of the motive of the drafters of the Constitution does not answer the question of whether the Constitution established a desirable or justifiable form of government. Evaluation of the worth of the Constitution can, it would seem, be conducted quite independently of an awareness of the motives of the Founding Fathers.

The above three examples, therefore, tend to explain the way in which a conclusion was reached. In certain contexts they do not respond to the question of whether the conclusion is in fact justifiable. Just as these two kinds of questions can be roughly distinguished, so the factors that led to the "discovery" of the conclusion can be differentiated from the process by which it is to be justified. I will refer to the procedure by which a conclusion is reached as the *process of discovery,* and to the procedure by which a conclusion is justified as the *process of justification.*

Having succeeded in establishing a rigid dichotomy between these two procedures, we must indicate three ways in which they may be related in actual practice. In the first place it should be evident that there is nothing immutable about any particular process of discovery or justification. Various procedures of discovery are possible; so too are various processes of justification. In both instances the procedure may be highly ordered or formalized, or it may be quite unsystematic and haphazard. When the procedure has a regular pattern that is systematically employed in each instance of discovery or justification, it might be called a "logic of discovery" or a "logic of justification," the word "logic" denoting precisely that attribute of order of procedure.

In the second place, for any given conjunction of a process of discovery and a process of justification an asymmetrical relationship obtains between them. That is to say, a procedure of discovery may be adopted if it succeeds in "generating" more conclusions that can be justified within the accepted logic of justification than any other discovery procedure. In a real sense the logic of justification provides the criteria by which both particular conclusions and the procedures of discovery may be evaluated; it is not easy to see how the converse could be true for any logic of discovery.

And finally, it would be a mistake to conclude that because two separable procedures are involved, they are not usually performed by the same individual. Indeed, although it is not always true, it is generally assumed that one should not put forward a conclusion or act upon a decision until one has subjected it to, and substantiated it by, one's logic of justification. This is perhaps what is meant by *rational behavior.*

I have labored this point both because it is one that is seldom appreciated by legal philosophers and because it is directly relevant to many of the theories that concern themselves with the nature of legal reasoning. For if someone talks about the legal decision process, he might be seeking to ask the kinds of questions that are relevant to an understanding of what I have called the process of discovery. But he might also be endeavoring to pose questions which relate to the procedure of justification that was employed. I think that at least some of the legal philosophers discussed above have tended to ask plausible questions about discovery. Those who have stressed the inadequacies of the deductive theory and who have sought to substitute some other description in its place have perhaps shed much light upon the discovery procedures used by the courts. By equating the process of discovery with the process of decision, they have argued quite persuasively that the judge's *opinion* is surely not an accurate report of the decision process. And indeed, if the decision process is coextensive with the process of discovery, it is probable that they are correct.

But it is, I think, chimerical to suppose that most judicial opinions purport to describe the process of discovery. Surely the kind of reasoning process that is evidenced by the usual judicial opinion is more suggestive of a typical justificatory procedure. Turning by way of analogy to the example of the scientist—it is one thing to read a judicial opinion as a report of why or how the judge "hit upon" the decision and quite another thing to read the opinion as an account of the procedure he employed in "testing" it. To insist—as many legal philosophers appear to have done—that a judicial opinion is an accurate description of the decision process there employed if and only if it faithfully describes the procedure of discovery is to help to *guarantee* that the opinion will be found wanting. But if the opinion is construed to be a report of the justificatory procedure employed by the judge, then the not infrequent reliance upon such things as rules of law and rules of logic seems more plausible. For conceivably, at least, some judges have felt that before they render a decision in a case they must be able to justify that decision. They may have had a hunch that a particular decision would be "right," they may have had a grudge against a particular defendant or plaintiff, but they might also have felt that considerations of this kind do not count as justifications for rendering a binding judicial decision, and that unless they could justify the decision "they would like to give" by appealing to certain other criteria, the decision ought not to be handed down as binding upon the litigants. And it may just be that some judges have thought they must be able to establish a formally valid relationship between the decision and certain more general premises, and be able also to give good reasons for the premises so selected. If this is so, then the attacks upon the deductive theory are not wrong; they are simply irrelevant.

It is sometimes urged that simply because courts use a deductive procedure as a procedure of justification, the adherence to such a procedure must be an ineffectual means of restricting the kinds of decisions that courts can appropriately render. As is so often true, it is very difficult to tell exactly what the objection is or how to refute it. Jerome Frank, for example, seems hopelessly equivocal on this point. He asserts, and I think wholly correctly, that there is a sense in which judging of all kinds begins "with a conclusion more or less vaguely formed; a man ordinarily starts with such a conclusion and afterwards tries to find premises which will substantiate it. If he cannot, to his satisfaction, find proper arguments, . . . he will, unless he is arbitrary or mad, reject the conclusion and seek another." This is roughly what I mean by *justification*. But then Frank goes on to say just as emphatically that "There is no rule by which you can predict when he will verbalize his conclusion in the form of a new rule, or by which he can determine when to consider a case as an exception to an old rule, or by which he can make up his mind whether to select one or another old rule to explain or guide his judgment. His decision is primary, the rules he may happen to refer to are incidental."

Now, it is surely difficult to reconcile these two passages. In the first one Frank implies quite strongly that there are or might be criteria which would force a person to reject a conclusion which had been tentatively formed. Yet, in the second he insists that there is no explanation which a judge could give for having appealed to one rule rather than to another as the justification for his decision. Again, a few pages later Frank says, "We have seen that one of their [legal rules' and principles'] chief uses is to enable the judges to give formal justifications—rationalizations—of the conclusions at which they otherwise arrive." Here, as elsewhere, Frank appears to equate the process of justification with the process of rationalization. But surely, as he himself has admitted, these need not be the same. In fact, on the very next page, he observes that "the conscientious judge, having tentatively arrived at a conclusion, can check up to see whether such a conclusion, without unfair distortion of the facts, can be linked with the generalized points of view theretofore acceptable. If none such are discoverable, he is forced to consider more acutely whether his tentative conclusion is wise, both with respect to the case before him and with respect to possible implications for future cases."

Frank sometimes seems to be saying that all justification is necessarily rationalization (in the currently accepted connotation of the term), that a reason can always be given for a conclusion, and that therefore the requirement that judges justify their decisions can never have any effect upon the decisions they will render. Just as often, however, he appears to be suggesting that judges have not tried to justify their decisions very conscientiously, that they have been content with mere rationalization, and that they ought to adhere to stricter canons of justification which are, apparently, capable of formulation.

These are, however, two dramatically different theses, and they must be kept distinct. If justifications are necessarily mere rationalizations, then there is little utility in worrying about the kinds of justification which ought to be required. But if the acceptance of criteria of justification could make a difference in the decisions which a court would render, then the specification and evaluation of alternative criteria is a significant undertaking. . . .

. . . If the talk about judicial hunches, emotions, and personalities relates to questions of discovery, it need not be inconsistent with a wholly different analysis concerning procedures of justification. Thus I do suggest that questions pertaining to justification can usefully be kept distinct from questions about discovery. And I propose finally that there do not seem to be any very persuasive reasons for believing that the adoption of some procedures of justification could not have an important effect upon the way in which courts decide particular cases.

## QUESTIONS

1. Compare Wasserstrom's discussion of judicial justification with the following excerpt about discovery and justification in science:

> The scientist who discovers a theory is usually guided to his discovery by guesses; he cannot name a method by means of which he found the theory and can only say that it appeared plausible to him, that he had the right hunch, or that he saw intuitively which assumption would fit the facts. Some philosophers have misunderstood this psychological description of discovery as proving that there exists no logical relation leading from the facts to the theory. . . . Inductive in-

ference is for them guesswork inaccessible to logical analysis. These philosophers do not see that the same scientist who discovered his theory through guessing presents it to others only after he sees that his guess is justified by the facts. It is this claim of justification in which the scientist performs an inductive inference, since he wishes to say not only that the facts are derivable from his theory, but also that the facts make his theory probable and recommend it for the prediction of further observational facts. The inductive inference is employed not for finding a theory, but for justifying it in terms of observational data. . . .

The act of discovery escapes logical analysis; there are no logical rules in terms of which a "discovery machine" could be constructed that would take over the creative function of the genius. But it is not the logician's task to account for scientific discoveries; all he can do is to analyze the relation between given facts and a theory presented to him with the claim that it explains these facts. In other words, logic is concerned only with the context of justification. And the justification of a theory in terms of observational data is the subject of the theory of induction.*

2.  The claim that judges' decisions are influenced by personal predilections, political outlook, and so on, is extremely plausible and probably true. If so, does this claim undercut Wasserstrom's critique of Frank?

## Priestley v. Fowler (1837)†

Priestley v. Fowler *is an important case because it has been used as an example of how judicial decision making is influenced by class bias. The case has been viewed as an effort by the House of Lords (the highest appellate court in England) to support the rights of the wealthy, ruling class over those of the working class. This view is espoused in the upcoming excerpt from Harold Laski and criticized in the excerpt by Roscoe Pound.*

Priestley v. Fowler *involved a butcher's employee (the "servant") who was given the task of delivering goods in a van. While the employee was performing this duty, the van broke down. The accident caused the employee to fall to the ground and suffer a fractured thigh. The employee then sued the butcher (the "master"), alleging that the butcher had a legal duty to make sure that the van was safe and since the van was not safe the butcher was responsible for the injury.*

Before *Priestley v. Fowler was decided, it had been established that a master was liable to an outside party injured by the negligence of the master's servant acting in the course of his employment. This is the doctrine of* respondeat superior, *literally, "let the principal be responsible." The plaintiff in* Priestley v. Fowler *sought to extend this doctrine so that the master would also be held liable for an injury* suffered by the servant *in the course of his employment.* Priestley v. Fowler *has traditionally been considered to have introduced the "fellow servant rule." This is the idea that the*

---

* Hans Reichenbach, *The Rise of Scientific Philosophy* (Berkeley and Los Angeles: University of California Press, 1951), pp. 230-231.

† 3 Mees & Wels. 1 (Exchequer, 1837).

*employer is not liable for an injury to one employee caused by another employee in the course of their employment. However, this interpretation of the case has been questioned. As Francis Headon Newark notes, there was no allegation by the plaintiff in Priestley v. Fowler "about the act of any fellow servant or indeed any suggestion that the duty sought to be put on the employer was other than a primary duty to ensure that the van was a safe conveyance."*

*Sharp criticism of the economic interpretation of the case came from Pound. He argued that this decision was not an expression of the judges' class bias but rather that it reflected a legal trend of the time: the emancipation of workers from being viewed as dependents of their masters. Pound argued that the dependency relationship was being replaced by a contract relationship. Workers were increasingly considered to be contracting for the use of their labor. Thus Pound's argument was in part that the court decided that the master could not be held liable for the servant's injury because (as the Court stated in presenting the issue), "no contract, and therefore no duty, can be implied on the part of the master to cause the servant to be safely and securely carried."*

CHIEF BARON, LORD ABINGER, delivered the judgment of the Court.

. . . It is admitted that there is no precedent for the present action by a servant against a master. We are therefore to decide the question upon general principles, and in doing so we are at liberty to look at the consequences of a decision the one way or the other.

If the master be liable to the servant in this action, the principle of that liability will be found to carry us to an alarming extent. He who is responsible by his general duty, or by the terms of this contract, for all the consequences of negligence in a matter in which he is the principal, is responsible for the negligence of all his inferior agents. If the owner of the carriage is therefore responsible for the sufficiency of this carriage to his servant, he is responsible for the negligence of his coach-maker, or his harness-maker, or his coachman. The footman, therefore, who rides behind the carriage, may have an action against his master for a defect in the carriage, owing to the negligence of the coachmaker, or for a defect in the harness arising from the negligence of the harness-maker, or for drunkenness, neglect, or want of skill in the coachman; nor is there any reason why the principle should not, if applicable in this class of cases, extend to many others. The master, for example, would be liable to the servant for the negligence of the chambermaid, for putting him into a damp bed; for that of the upholsterer, for sending in a crazy bedstead, whereby he was made to fall down while asleep and injure himself; for the negligence of the cook, in not properly cleaning the copper vessels used in the kitchen; of the butcher, in supplying the family with meat of a quality injurious to the health; of the builder, for a defect in

* F.H. Newark, *Elegantia Juris* (Belfast: Northern Ireland Legal Quarterly, 1973), p. 145.

the foundation of the house, whereby it fell, and injured both the master and the servant by the ruins.

The inconvenience, not to say the absurdity of these consequences, affords a sufficient argument against the application of this principle to the present case. But, in truth, the mere relation of the master and the servant never can imply an obligation on the part of the master to take more care of the servant than he may reasonably be expected to do of himself. He is, no doubt, bound to provide for the safety of his servant in the course of his employment, to the best of his judgement, information, and belief. The servant is not bound to risk his safety in the service of his master, and may, if he thinks fit, decline any service in which he reasonably apprehends injury to himself: and in most of the cases in which danger may be incurred, if not in all, he is just as likely to be acquainted with the probability and extent of it as the master. In that sort of employment, especially, which is described in the declaration in this case, the plaintiff must have known as well as his master, and probably better, whether the van was sufficient, whether it was overloaded, and whether it was likely to carry him safely. In fact, to allow this sort of action to prevail would be an encouragement to the servant to omit that diligence and caution which he is in duty bound to exercise on the behalf of his master, to protect him against the misconduct or negligence of others who serve him, and which diligence and caution, while they protect the master, are a much better security against any injury the servant may sustain by the negligence of others engaged under the same master, than any recourse against his master for damages could possibly afford.

## QUESTIONS

In his opinion, Lord Abinger states: "The inconvenience, not to say the absurdity of these consequences, affords a sufficient argument against the application of this principle to the present case."

1. To what "principle" is he referring?
2. To what "consequences" is he referring?
3. Are the "consequences" so absurd?

## *Harold J. Laski,*
## *Class Bias In Judicial Decision Making (1935)* *

*Harold Laski (1893-1950) was a teacher, political activist, and theoretician of the British Labor party. He taught at Harvard from 1916 to 1920. Among his friends were*

* Harold J. Laski, *The State in Theory and Practice* (New York: Viking Press, Penguin, 1935), pp. 161-162, 168, 173-174, 175-177, 183. Copyright 1935 by Harold J. Laski. Copyright renewed 1963 by Frida Laski. Reprinted by permission of Viking Penguin Inc.

*Justice Felix Frankfurter and Justice Oliver Wendell Holmes. Laski's political views drifted steadily over the years from a democratic socialist orientation toward Marxism. He eventually accepted the Marxist notion that the contradictions and class biases inherent in capitalist societies doom capitalism to failure. The following excerpt comes from Laski's period of transition to a Marxist world view. Laski uses the case of* Priestley v. Fowler *as an example of how the legal system serves the interests of the ruling class. Here, he argues that such a situation is inevitable in any society in which lawyers and judges have lifelong associations with the powerful elite.*

I have pointed out that every society is the theatre of a conflict between economic classes for a larger material benefit, for, that is, a larger share in the results to be distributed from the productive process. Since the power to produce within any society is dependent upon peace, the state must maintain law and order to that end. But, in so doing, it is necessarily maintaining the law and order implied in the particular system of class-relations of which it is the expression. In feudal society, that is, the law and order which the state maintains is the law and order necessary to the preservation of feudal principles. In a capitalist society, the state maintains the law and order necessary to preserve capitalist principles. . . . The state, that is to say, is always at the disposal of that class in the community in which is vested the legal title to the ownership of instruments of production. The law it makes will be law for their interest. The ownership it maintains will be their ownership. If the number of owners, therefore, in a state be few, the bias of the law will be towards the interest of that few. . . .

This view was compressed by the Communist Manifesto into a famous sentence. "The executive of the modern state," wrote Marx and Engels, "is simply a committee for managing the common affairs of the bourgeoisie. . . ."

. . . We do not need to argue that all law is a product of the class-struggle. It is clear enough that a good deal of law, in commercial matters, for instance, and, even more, in procedure, represents principles quite remote from it. But it is equally clear, I think, that the idea of the class-struggle permeates legal notions at every point of pivotal importance. . . .

Nor must we forget the fact that wealth is a decisive factor in the power to take advantage of the opportunities the law affords its citizens to protect their rights. The ability to undertake an action in the courts, even with the provision made for legal aid to the poor, remains a grim financial question, and, on the civil side of the law, with its massive hierarchy of appeals, the advantage is solidly with the rich. Broadly, there is equality before the law only when the price of admission to its opportunities can be equally paid; and there is no administrative equity to redress this balance. It is simply inherent in a society with the class-relations of our own. And it is those class-relations also which mean that, as a general rule, the ablest lawyers will be at the service of those only who are able to afford them. The successful lawyer—the class from which, in the Anglo-American system, the members of the judiciary are mostly drawn—spends his life in ministering to the dominating class of our society. It is wholly natural, therefore, that he should come, as a general rule, to share its outlook, that his intellectual influence, therefore, should largely be exercised on its behalf. It is a sound instinct that has persuaded the working-classes to look upon the legal profession as one of the protective ramparts of conservatism.

I am not, it must be noted, in any way or in any degree challenging the good will of the lawyer or the legal system. I am merely saying that once the postulates of the society in which they function imply inequality, the main burden of their influence should be towards maintaining it. And when, as with ourselves, so large a part of law is rooted in precedent, it is natural for the lawyer's mind to dwell upon continuity with the past rather than departure from it. Judge-made law is rarely innovating law unless, as with the work of Chief Justice Holt and Lord Mansfield, it deals with a situation in which the guiding precedents are few or non-existent; and where the lawyer, as with Chief Justice Marshall, or Lord Abinger in Priestley v. Fowler, confronts an experiment in which the rights of property are in serious hazard, the emphasis of his work will always tend to be towards supporting them rather than attacking them. That is surely why most great movements for legal reform have either come from outside the profession altogether, or from members of it who, like Bentham, have had a very peripheral connection with it. The business of a legal system is to make the postulates of a society work. It would be remarkable indeed if it could be so worked as to secure their fundamental transformation. . . .

. . . Law, that is to say, is never impartial in the sense of being above the battle, or indifferent to the results which may emerge. The courts, on the contrary, are a fundamental instrument in that battle. They shape the contours of the society, more interstitially, perhaps, because less directly, than either the legislature or the executive; but they are bound to the same purpose. They give effect to the result of the conflicting class-antagonisms which shape the atmosphere in which they have to work.

## QUESTIONS

1. In the excerpt, Laski writes of "the postulates" of the society in which lawyers function. What are the "postulates" of American society?
2. What have been some of the major changes in the postulates of American society over the years?

3. Identify ways in which the legal system reflected, helped, or hindered these changes.

4. How would one go about investigating whether the class-bias theory of judicial decision making is correct or not?

## Roscoe Pound, "The Economic Interpretation and the Law of Torts" (1940) *

*Roscoe Pound (1870-1964) was a prolific scholar. He served as dean of the Harvard Law School from 1916 to 1936. His early writings furnished support for legal reforms that included juvenile court legislation and workmen's compensation. Pound believed that law was a means of social control and that legislators should recognize the interplay among law and other forms of social control. He saw the legal system as a means of balancing social interests. In this excerpt from a 1940 law review article, Pound disputes the contention that court decisions can always be explained as attempts to support the economically dominant class. He traces the history of the doctrine of* respondeat superior *(defined in the headnote to* Priestley v. Fowler) *and contends that the decision in* Priestley v. Fowler *was consistent with legal and social change under way at the time.*

With an economic interpretation of the general course of history and so of legal history one can have no quarrel. Nor within limits can one quarrel with such an interpretation of certain types of events in legal history. What must give us pause is making it the sole weapon in the jurist's armory or the sole instrument in his tool chest; the reference of every item in the judicial process, of every single decision and every working out of a legal precept by applying the technique of the law to the received materials of decision, to the operation, conscious or unconscious, of the desires and self-interest of an economically dominant class.

Undoubtedly what the proponents of the economic interpretation see behind all law is behind many laws framed by legislative law-makers. The legislator is not trained in a technique of referring his action to general principles. He has no settled habits of applying an authoritative technique to authoritatively given materials. Much of legislation can be explained very well by the economic interpretation as developed by our American juristic realists. Yet one has only to read colonial legislation as to certain religious

* Roscoe Pound, *"The Economic Interpretation and the Law of Torts,"* Harvard Law Review, 53 (1940), pp. 365, 366-367, 373-383. Copyright ©1940 by The Harvard Law Review Association. A *tort* is a civil (noncriminal) wrong, other than breach of contract, for which the law provides a remedy. There are three elements in tort liability: (1) existence of a legal duty, (2) breach of the duty by the defendant, and (3) damage or injury suffered by the plaintiff as a result of the breach of duty.

sects (to take an example which cannot be controversial today) in order to see that even legislation need have no economic explanation but may go on deep-seated beliefs or prejudices quite apart from economic considerations. Arbitrary legislative precepts are fitted into the traditional system by interpretation and application. The taught tradition of law is little affected by such details. What stands out in the history of Anglo-American law is the resistance of the taught tradition in the hands of judges drawn from any class you like, so they have been trained in the tradition, against all manner of economically or politically powerful interests. It is not that economic power has dictated decision of particular cases or judicial promulgation of particular rules, but rather that economic progress has led to new wants, new claims, new demands, new desires.

Does it follow that single decisions are shaped by class interest? Does the economic status of the parties determine the action of the courts in particular cases? Are legal reasoning, doctrinal exposition, systematic development of authoritative starting points for reasoned decisions mere pretense, mere camouflage of results reached apart from reason solely on the basis of class interest or the social and economic position of the respective parties?

Law is neither wholly reason nor wholly experience. It is experience developed by reason, and reason checked and directed by experience. The strongest single influence both in determining single decisions and in guiding a course of decision is a taught tradition of logically interdependent precepts and of referring cases to principles. Admittedly there are often competing precepts, competing principles, competing starting points for legal reasoning, often of equal authority. It is here that the ideal element in law comes into play, since the results of choosing one starting point rather than another are measured by the received social ideal, as it has been taught to judges and lawyers. The effect of economic changes upon this ideal is for the most part gradual and slow, no matter what class is affected. The business man and the leader of industry have had quite as much cause for complaint in this respect as the labor leader; and the farmer, long dominant in American politics, no less than either. As Maitland puts it, "taught law is tough law." . . .

Let us see what the proponents of the economic interpretation vouch for their doctrine. Their stock in trade is Priestley v. Fowler, 3 M. & W. 1 (Ex. 1837). A typical pronouncement may be found in Walter Lippmann's *Good Society* [p. 188]. He says: "Under the old common law of England a workman who was injured could sue the master for damages. If he had been injured by a fellow workman's negligence, he could still sue the master because the law held the master liable for his servant's acts. Under this system of law the state was ready to intervene on behalf of an injured workman and recover damages for him from his employer. In 1837 this system of law was changed in a decision rendered by Lord Abinger. After that, it became the law that the master was not liable for an injury to a working man when the injury was due to a fellow working man." For this positive statement he cites an article in the Encyclopaedia of the Social Sciences. But neither Mr. Lippmann nor the writer in the Encyclopaedia cites or could cite a decision in the English-speaking world before 1837 on the point in question, much less one holding the master liable in such a case.

. . . When, however, we read the case we note that it was brought and argued and decided on a contract theory; a theory of what was and what was not implied in a contract of employment. The declaration averred a duty to cause the plaintiff to be safely and securely carried on the wagon of the butcher whose employee he was. The wagon had been overloaded by a fellow employee. The court said that the butcher was not bound to take more care of his servant than he did of himself and that the servant must have known better than his master that the load was too heavy. It is a safe conjecture that in 1837 the butcher and the boy working for him, who presently as he learned the business would set up for himself as a master butcher, were or would be regarded by the court as of the same class. We cannot assume that the court thought of the case in terms of a packing company of today and a laborer, one of some hundreds in the plant.

Mr. Lippmann's version of *Priestley v. Fowler* proceeds on three false assumptions: (1) That *respondeat superior* is a universal principle of justice, generally recognized as such; (2) that *respondeat superior* is a general principle of law, to be developed and applied wherever the relation of employer and employee exists; (3) that prior to that case it was recognized as applying to hold the master not only for injuries to third persons but also for injuries to his servants without his fault. . . .

"If the law went no further," says Mr. Justice Holmes, "than to declare a man liable for the consequences of acts specifically commanded by him, with knowledge of the circumstances under which those consequences were the natural results of those acts, it would need no explanation and would introduce no new principle." The new principle requiring explanation, he goes on to say, was introduced into the law when the master without fault was treated as if he were the tortfeasor.* There was an old historical liability for the acts of those who were in the household as dependents. In the frankpledge system† there was this sort of liability for the acts of others.

---

* *A tortfeasor* is someone who commits a tort (defined on page 28).
† In old English (feudal) law the *frankpledge* was the guarantee made to the sovereign by all the members of a group. They pledged to behave properly and be responsible for one another's conduct.

The master was made to stand as security for the conduct of his servants, to hand them over to justice or pay the fine himself. So far was this carried that the host was liable for the tort of a guest in his house as well as for wrongs done by his servant. Thus liability of the master for the torts of a servant comes down from a primitive liability of the head of a household to buy off the vengeance of the injured person or surrender the wrongdoing dependent.... A historical liability for those who were in the household was made into a liability for the acts of nondependent employees in order to maintain the general security. But as to fellow servants the idea has not been one of maintaining the general security. It has been one of insuring those who were in no economic position to bear loss at the expense of the nearest person at hand who could bear it. This is a very recent conception as to the requirements of justice, quite out of line with nineteenth-century ideas and one which the judges of 1837 could not reasonably have been expected to grasp. At that time the idea of using litigation as a means to insure what Professor Patten calls bringing about a distribution of the economic surplus had not occurred to any one.

As I said above, throughout the law there is a problem of reconciling the general security and the individual life, using the latter term to mean the fullest and freest exercise and development of his powers by each individual. When we seek to maintain justice, as the ideal relation between men, and impose liability to the measure of that ideal, we are continually given pause by the exigencies of the general security. Hence in the law of torts there is a constant quest of practical adjustment between the two principles; on the one hand the principle of responsibility for culpable conduct, and on the other hand the principle of responsibility as a means of maintaining the general security. . . .

. . . In the nature of the problem of adjusting human relations there must be this twofold basis of a law of torts. The most that has ever been achieved is a practical balance between the two principles. The only guide to adjustment seems to be to give effect to as much of each as we may with the least infringement of the other. But this had not been learned till long after 1837. At that time, liability without fault was taken to be an obsolete institution of primitive societies.

Equally it would have been too much to expect in 1837, when the whole thought of the time was moving away from thinking of employer and employee as a domestic relation, that a court would hark back to that conception in order to require an employer to answer for the safety of the employee in matters where the employer was in no wise at fault. In general, one has a duty to protect those whom the law makes dependent upon him. But the traditional technique of the law is to generalize and refer cases to principles so as to bring about a body of logically interdependent precepts. When employees were asserting their independence and a contract idea was taking them out of the category of domestic dependents, no common-law court could have been found, of whomsoever composed, to turn back to the old dependent idea and impose a liability to take care of the employee on that basis. Workmen's Compensation depends upon a wholly different conception of liability from that entertained by any one in the first half of the nineteenth century. Understand me. I am not arguing for the fellow servant rule as something that should be restored or as something that should have been preserved in the law under the conditions of today. I am simply showing that it was not a setting up of an arbitrary exception to a universally recognized principle of justice. It was not a reversal of a settled proposition of law. It was not inconsistent with the prior course of decision. It was not something adopted willfully in 1837 by a tribunal consciously expressing in legal doctrine the self interest of a dominant social or economic class. The conception of the employer-employee relation as a domestic relation, which is at the bottom of tort liability of the employer for the fault of the employee, is, as Mr. Justice Holmes has shown, also at the bottom of the fellow servant rule which is charged with being an arbitrary exception to it.

An exclusively economic interpretation of single decisions and single items of judicial action leaves out of account the tenacity of a taught tradition. It takes no account of the instinctive tendency of the lawyer to refer every case back to some general principle. It ignores the prevailing mode of thought of the time which often reflects an economic situation of the past when the taught ideal was formative. Specifically in the cases we have been considering it ignores the nineteenth-century attempt to reduce liability to contract and culpable causation of harm. In 1882 this founding of liability upon undertaking and fault seemed to Mr. Justice Holmes the common sense view. No speculation as to class bias is needed to explain how common-law judges of that time in general, where not bound by authority, thought likewise.

## QUESTIONS

1.  Identify Pound's argument against the class-bias theory of judicial decision making.
2.  Are Pound and Laski in complete disagreement?
3.  In a portion of the opinion from *Roberson v. Rochester Folding Box Co.* (that is omitted from the excerpt in the next chapter) the court quotes the following statement from another decision: "It was not our intention to

decide any case but the one before us. . . . If, as sometimes happens, broader statements were made by way of argument or otherwise than were essential to the decisions of the questions presented, they are the dicta of the writer of the opinion and not the decision of the court. A judicial opinion . . . is only binding so far as it is relevant, and when it wanders from the point at issue it no longer has the force of an official utterance." In the light of this quotation and Pound's analysis of *Priestley v. Fowler*, where might it be said that Lord Abinger's opinion "wandered" from the point at issue?

# II

# *Types of Legal Argument*

It is useful to begin this chapter with the reminder that an argument, as we are using the term, consists minimally of a least two statements, of which one (the premise) is offered as a reason for accepting the other (the conclusion). Most actual arguments, of course, contain a number of premises that, taken together, are assumed to justify the conclusion. A piece of argumentative discourse can be even more complex, for it may contain a series of arguments, such that the conclusion of one argument is used as a premise in another argument. This is often the case in judicial reasoning, in which a judge may present an argument that is designed to establish that some given proposition is a rule of law and then uses that proposition (by applying it to the facts of the case) in justifying the final decision. In reading any judicial opinion it is important—although not always easy—to identify the premises and conclusions of the various arguments. Later in this chapter a few opinions are analyzed in detail. The ultimate aim is to be able to evaluate judicial arguments, to distinguish the good from the bad and the better from the worse. At the very least, if one finds some argument unconvincing, one wants to be able to account for that fact. To this end, it is necessary to distinguish *types* of argument.

Types of argument may be distinguished in two ways: first, by their *form* or *structure,* and second, by the *kinds of reasons* offered for the conclusions. The study of argument from both of these perspectives has a tradition that goes back to Aristotle, but the first is much more developed and far less controversial than the second. The opening part of this chapter will concentrate on form. The purpose, however, is not to survey even the most frequently used forms of argument. It is, rather, to achieve the idea of logical form, the distinction between deductive and nondeductive arguments, and some of the logical characteristics associated with them. (For many readers this portion of this discussion will be merely a review.) Both legal and nonlegal examples will be given. Some of the special features of legal arguments will also be disclosed.

## Two Perspectives: An Interpretation

Before turning to this task, it seems appropriate to illustrate briefly the two perspectives on the study of argument: the perspective of form and the perspective of the kinds of reasons offered for conclusions. Let us consider the case of *Lubitz v. Wells.*

The issue before the court in this case was whether the plaintiff had a "cause of action." A cause of action is a set of alleged facts that, if proven, is grounds for judicial relief. In other words, if the plaintiff proves his allegations, he will show he has suffered a legal wrong that the court can remedy. (Other cases that will be considered later also involve the question whether a "cause of action" exists.)

However, in *Lubitz v. Wells* the defendant claimed that the facts alleged by the plaintiff (even if all were proven) were insufficient to state a cause of action. This claim was made in a motion called a *demurrer.* When the defendant prevails in a demurrer (as he did in *Lubitz v. Wells*), the plaintiff's complaint is dismissed.

In this case, the plaintiff claimed that James Wells, Sr., was negligent by leaving his golf club in his yard where Wells's son picked it up, swung it, and injured Judith Lubitz. Negligence is a legal standard of culpability. It means the failure to exercise the degree of care that a "reasonably prudent person" would have used under similar circumstances, by doing something that the reasonably prudent person would not have done under the circumstances or by failing to do something that the reasonably prudent person would have done. Here is the judge's opinion:

### LUBITZ v. WELLS (1955)[1]

JUDGE TROLAND:
> The complaint alleges that James Wells was the owner of a golf club and that he left it for some time lying on the ground in the backyard of his home. That thereafter his son, the defendant James Wells, Jr., aged eleven years, while playing in the yard with the plaintiff, Judith Lubitz, aged nine years, picked up the

[1] 19 Conn. Supp. 322, 113 A.2d 147 (1955).

golf club and proceeded to swing at a stone lying on the ground. In swinging the golf club, James Wells, Jr., caused the club to strike the plaintiff about the jaw and chin.

Negligence alleged against the young Wells boy is that he failed to warn his little playmate of his intention to swing the club and that he did swing the club when he knew she was in a position of danger.

In an attempt to hold the boy's father, James Wells, liable for his son's action, it is alleged that James Wells was negligent because although he knew the golf club was on the ground in his backyard and that his children would play with it, and that although he knew or "should have known" that the negligent use of the golf club by children would cause injury to a child, he neglected to remove the golf club from the backyard or to caution James Wells, Jr., against the use of the same.

The demurrer challenges the sufficiency of the allegations of the complaint to state a cause of action or to support a judgment against the father, James Wells.

It would hardly be good sense to hold that this golf club is so obviously and intrinsically dangerous that it is negligence to leave it lying on the ground in the yard. The father cannot be held liable on the allegations of this complaint. [Citations omitted.]

The demurrer is sustained.

The main argumentative part of this opinion consists of two sentences. Like many other judges, Judge Troland does not spell out the argument, so we are given the job of reconstructing it. We might do this as follows:

(i)   The father can be held liable <u>only if</u> it is negligence to leave the golf club lying on the ground.

(ii)  It is negligence to leave the golf club lying on the ground <u>only if</u> the golf club is so obviously and intrinsically [a] dangerous [object].

(iii) But it is not the case that the golf club is so obviously and intrinsically [a] dangerous [object](because it would hardly be good sense to so hold <u>it</u>).

(iv)  Therefore, the father cannot be held liable.

It will be noticed that statements (i) and (ii) are each compound statements that are formed by joining together two statements with the connective <u>only if</u>. Statement (iii) is the *denial* of the consequent part of (ii), and the <u>reason</u> for the denial is stated in the parentheses. The form of the argument can best be seen if we use letters as symbols. Let

*L* stand for "The father can be held liable,"
*N* stand for "It is negligence to leave the golf club lying on the ground," and
*D* stand for "The golf club is so obviously and intrinsically [a] dangerous [object]."

Putting aside the parenthetical "because" clause, which gives a reason for rejecting one of the other statements in the argument (D), the *form* of the argument can now be rendered as

(i)   *L* only if *N*.
(ii)  *N* only if *D*.
(iii) It is not the case that *D*.
(iv)  Therefore, it is not the case that *L*.

This argument is a complex form of the argument form known as *modus tollens*:

*P* only if *Q*.
It is not the case that *Q*.
Therefore, it is not the case that *P*,

where *P* and *Q* stand for any statements.

From the perspective of form, Judge Troland's argument, as reconstructed, is valid: if each of the three premises (i), (ii), and (iii) is true (or correct), the conclusion is also true (or correct). The three premises, taken together, justify the conclusion (iv).

In our example the "because" clause states a reason for rejecting some other statement, *D*, which in turn leads to the rejection of *N*. Judge Troland seems to be maintaining that the acceptance of *N* would require accepting a consequence, *D*, that is absurd or contrary to "good sense," so *N* must be rejected (and, therefore, so also *L*). From the perspective of the *kind of reason* given by the judge, one can say that the argument is an "appeal to good sense." Judge Troland is presuming that the law, or judgments made by judges in their rulings, should make good sense. (Of course, he has not spelled out what this means, and his rejection of *D* might be disputed.) Judge Troland's specific argument, in a way, makes a negative appeal to good sense. Viewing his argument as a whole, one may say that it is a variety of a *practical reductio ad absurdum*, which is very frequently used by judges: if a purported rule, judgment, or decision would have unacceptable consequences, then the rule, judgment, or decision should be rejected.[2]

Enough has been said to give the reader an idea of the distinction between the study of arguments from the perspective of form and their study from the perspective of the kinds of reasons given for a conclusion. The two perspectives are of course complementary, and both are required for an understanding of legal reasoning. There is still much to be said about each.

---

[2] Premise (iii) may also be represented as the conclusion of an argument:
 A ruling should be accepted only if the ruling would make good sense.
 Ruling *D* would not make good sense.
 Therefore, *D* should not be accepted.
In our reconstruction of Judge Troland's argument, the conclusion appears as "It is not the case that *D*."

## Forms of Argument

Let us now turn to a summary discussion of forms of argument. Examples will be used to illustrate the ideas of logical form and formal validity, and also the idea of deductive and nondeductive arguments. Consider the following (nonlegal) argument:

>    (1)   All ruminants are mammals.
>    (2)   All elks are ruminants.
>    (3)   Therefore, all elks are mammals.

Using capital letters as symbols for the above statements, this argument will be seen to have the form

>    (1′)   $A$
>    (2′)   $B$
>    (3′)   Therefore, $C$

which corresponds to a hypothetical sentence of the form

If $A$ and $B$, then $C$.

Every argument, in fact, corresponds to a hypothetical sentence of the form

If $R$, then $C$

in which $R$ stands for the conjunction of all the reasons or premises (or the premise, in case there is only one) of the particular argument and $C$ stands for its conclusion. But the argument above also has a more complex internal structure, which may be schematically represented as follows:

>    (1″)   All $X$ are $Y$.
>    (2″)   All $Z$ are $X$.
>    (3″)   Therefore, all $Z$ are $Y$.

It will readily be seen that *any* argument of this form (in which $X$, $Y$, and $Z$ are uniformly substituted by the appropriate nouns or noun phrases) is a *formally valid* argument. The formal validity of an argument does not depend on the truth of the premises. It means only that the conclusion logically *follows from* the premises; which is to say that *if* all the premises are true, the conclusion must also be true. The rules for constructing formally valid arguments are designed to be truth-preserving in this way.

The three statements can also be used to illustrate an *invalid* form of argument:

> (3)  All elks are mammals.
> (2)  All elks are ruminants.
> (1)  Therefore, all ruminants are mammals.

Here, the premises and the conclusion are all true, but the conclusion does not follow from the premises. Schematically, this argument has the form

> (3″)  All $Z$ are $Y$.
> (2″)  All $Z$ are $X$.
> (1″)  Therefore, all $X$ are $Y$.

Clearly, this form of argument is not truth-preserving. The following is an *instance* of this invalid form:

All Swedes are Scandinavians.
All Swedes are humans.
Therefore, all humans are Scandinavians.

which has true premises and a false conclusion.

A formally valid argument that has true premises is said to be a *sound* argument. If an argument is sound, its conclusion must be true. In debate or discussion, therefore, an argument may be attacked in two ways: by attempting to show that one of its premises is false or by attempting to show that it is invalid. On the other hand, if one concedes the truth of the premises of a formally valid argument, one must also concede the truth of the conclusion—or be guilty of irrationality.

Here is a good place to mention that in actual argumentation, one often omits some of the premises—on the assumption that they are understood by one's audience or that they are too obvious to mention. An argument with a suppressed premise is called an *enthymeme* ("in the mind"). For instance, suppose someone were to argue

> (2)  All elks are ruminants.
> (3)  Therefore, all elks are mammals.

As stated, the argument is invalid, and premise (1) should be supplied in order to make it valid. Judicial arguments are often enthymematic, and one has the task of filling in the missing premise or premises. In general, the rule to be followed is to supply only true (or acceptable) premises and also the most plausible ones in the given context.

The gist of very many judicial opinions can be expressed as instances of the valid argument form we have been discussing, namely, the inference from (1 ″) and (2 ″) to (3 ″).[3] In *Baker v. Libbie* (1912),[4] Chief Justice Rugg in effect argues as follows:

One has the right to the fruit of one's labor (i.e., fruits of labor are the
 property of their authors).
Private correspondence is a fruit of the author's labor.
Therefore, private correspondence is the property of the author.

In this example, grammar requires the use of the singular "is" in the second premise and in the conclusion, instead of the plural "are," and the quantifier "all" is implied though omitted. The argument is valid, but the reader may not wish to grant that the first premise is acceptable without qualification (the reader may wish to exclude, for example, the fruits of hard theft). The gist of Judge Cardozo's more complex opinion in *MacPherson v. Buick Motor Co.* (1916)[5] can perhaps be formulated as follows:

Any manufacturer who negligently constructs an article that may be seen
 to be inherently dangerous to life and limb when so constructed is
 liable in damages for injuries resulting proximately.
A manufacturer who constructs an automobile so that the spokes on a
 wheel are defective is such a manufacturer.
Therefore, a manufacturer who constructs an automobile so that the
 spokes on a wheel are defective is liable in damages for injuries
resulting proximately.

The arguments of both Rugg and Justice Cardozo are instances of

   (1 ″) All $X$ are $Y$.
   (2 ″) All $Z$ are $X$.
   (3 ″) Therefore, all $Z$ are $Y$.

though effortful thought may be required to see that this is the case. (Cardozo's opinion is examined in detail in the next chapter.)

 Thus far we have been discussing arguments in which the premises claim

---

[3] The following two examples are from Paul E. Treusch, "The Syllogism," *in Readings in Jurisprudence,* ed. Jerome Hall, (Indianapolis Bobbs-Merrill, 1938), pp. 541-542.
[4] 210 Mass. 599 (1912).
[5] 217 N.Y. 382, 111 N.E. 1050 (1916).

to be *sufficient grounds* for accepting the conclusion. Such arguments are called *deductive* arguments. A "good" deductive argument is a sound argument: if (1) all the premises are true and (2) the argument is an instance of a valid form, then no additional premises are needed in order to establish the truth of the conclusion. If either of these conditions should fail, the premises are not sufficient to establish the truth of the conclusion, and the argument is a "bad" deductive argument. Since a deductive argument purports to be sufficient to establish its conclusion as true, there is no middle ground between a good and a bad deductive argument. In a good deductive argument, the truth of the premises logically entails the truth of the conclusion.

There are, of course, very many other valid forms of argument besides the one on which most of our attention has just been focused. (Judge Troland's argument, as reconstructed, is an instance of such another valid form.) The point of the discussion has been to bring out certain logical ideas that will be needed for the analysis of legal reasoning, rather than to survey the main forms in general use. To complete this discussion let us now turn to *nondeductive* arguments. Again, our interest is to elicit certain logical ideas that will be needed for the subsequent analysis, so only two kinds of nondeductive argument will be taken up: induction by enumeration and argument by analogy. The field of nondeductive argument is highly problematic, and the account that follows is a simplified, skeletal treatment.

It is important to note in advance of this account that in deciding a question of law, a judge has to decide in effect, how a certain case or class of cases *ought* to be treated. This does not mean that such a judge would merely be expressing a personal opinion or making a moral judgment about how the case ought to be treated. For it is the judge's duty to decide how the case ought to be treated according to the law. (This is not to deny that moral considerations may enter into the judge's reasoning or that personal opinion can affect the decision.) Nevertheless, the conclusions of judicial arguments on questions of law, like the conclusions of moral arguments, are *normative* in character: they have "imperative" force and involve some notion of "what is right to do," whether according to law, morality, or some other kind of standard. Judicial conclusions thus are to be distinguished from conclusions in which no element of "oughtness" is explicit or implied; the latter conclusions are so-called descriptive statements. It is necessary to begin the account of nondeductive arguments with a discussion of *non*normative arguments. (Whether there is a sharp distinction between descriptive and normative statements—between *is* and *ought*—has been debated by philosophers. Still, it is a useful distinction in this context).[6]

---

[6] See W. D. Hudson (ed.), *The Is-Ought Question* (London: Macmillan, 1969).

In (nonnormative) nondeductive arguments, it is not claimed that the premises are sufficient to establish the truth of the conclusion but rather that the premises, if true, make the conclusion *more likely to be true than false*. Perhaps the main sorts of nondeductive arguments are the *inductive*. In these arguments, the premises are statements of what is usually called *evidence* for the conclusion; and, generally, the more evidence one has the more well supported the conclusion is—but it could still turn out to be false.

One kind of inductive argument is the induction by *enumeration*, in which the conclusion is a *generalization*. Suppose, for example, one has observed a number of white swans and has not observed swans of other color. One might then formulate the following argument:

> *a* is a swan and *a* is white.
> *b* is a swan and *b* is white.
> *c* is a swan and *c* is white.
>
> .
>
> .
>
> .
>
> *n* is a swan and *n* is white.
> ———————————————
> Therefore, all swans are white.

Here, the evidence consists of instances of the generalization, and more instances would tend to make the conclusion more reliable than otherwise. It is possible, therefore, to speak of "better or worse" inductive arguments.

Schematically, arguments of this kind have the following *form*:

> (i)   $x_1$ is F and $x_1$ is G.
> (ii)  $x_2$ is F and $x_2$ is G.
> (iii) $x_3$ is F and $x_3$ is G.
>
> .
>
> .
>
> .
>
> (n)   $x_n$ is F and $x_n$ is G.
> ———————————————
> Therefore, all F are G.

It should be clear that the truth of the conclusion is *not* guaranteed by the form of the argument (induction from instances to generalization) even when all the premises are true and no matter how numerous they are. (In our example, the generalization is in fact false, as Europeans discovered when they found black swans in Australia.) A good inductive argument—the criteria of which are problematic and not treatable here—can always be "improved" by the addition of premises that express further evidence. But it will not ensure that the conclusion is true, because the premises do not logically entail the conclusion. This feature puts nondeductive arguments, generally, in sharp contrast to good (i.e., sound) deductive arguments. In the latter, the truth of the conclusion is guaranteed by the form of the argument when the premises are true.

It is sometimes suggested that judges use arguments of this kind, induction by enumeration. That is, from the decision in a past case, or decisions in past cases, a judge might induce a general rule which governs the particular case that is before the court. Since such occurrences, however, may also be viewed as *arguments by analogy,* which are close relatives of induction by enumeration, the above suggestion will not be pursued. Arguments by analogy are important enough to merit a separate section, and the topic is also returned to in Chapter 3.

## Argument by Analogy

In order to grasp the form of analogical arguments it will be useful to look first at nonnormative examples. Again, the account will be skeletal.

Arguments by analogy proceed from certain given or *assumed resemblances* to an *inferred resemblance.* Such arguments are very frequently used in everyday life. A car dealer has to decide whether to hire a job applicant, Brown, as a salesman. The dealer argues from Brown's given resemblances to L, M, and N, who were previously hired as car salesmen and who turned out to be successful, that Brown will also be a successful car salesman: L, M, and N are graduates of Winsockie University, majored in physical education, and have good recommendations from their coaches; Brown is a graduate of Winsockie University, majored in physical education, and has good recommendations from his coaches; L, M, and N were successful car salesmen; therefore Brown will be a successful car salesman.

A classic example of analogical argument is given by the nineteenth-century logician W. Stanley Jevons:

> The planet Mars possesses an atmosphere, with clouds and mist closely resembling our own; it has seas distinguished from the land by a greenish color, and polar regions covered with snow. The red colour of the planet seems to be due to the atmosphere, like the red colour of our sunrises and sunsets. So much is similar in the surface of Mars and the surface of the Earth that we readily argue there must be inhabitants there as here.

The difference between analogical argument and induction by enumeration is that the inference depends not so much on the number of instances as on the resemblance of the compared items. It should be obvious that an argument by analogy, like induction by enumeration, at most establishes its conclusion as *more likely to be true than false.*

The *form* of arguments by analogy may be stated as

        (i)   *x* has characteristics F, G, . . .
        (ii)  *y* has characteristics F, G, . . .
        (iii) <u>*x* also has characteristic H.</u>
        (iv) Therefore, *y* has characteristic H.

In contrast to a good (i.e., sound) deductive argument, the form of a good analogical argument does not guarantee the truth of the conclusion even when all the premises are true. In other words, arguments by analogy are not formally valid; the falsity of the conclusion is compatible with the truth of the premises. There may be any number of respects in which Brown resembles the members of a group of successful ballet dancers (he and they like hot dogs, he and they know how to drive a car, etc., etc.), and an argument could be formulated that leads to the conclusion that Brown, too, will be a successful ballet dancer—but one would give it no credence.

It is extremely difficult to lay out strict criteria for a good analogical argument. Among the considerations that have to be taken into account in evaluating these arguments are such factors as the number of respects in which the compared objects resemble one another (positive analogies) and the number of respects in which they differ (negative analogies). Yet all this is very tricky. Again, there will be any number of respects in which Brown resembles L, M, and N (he and they like hot dogs, he and they play Ping-Pong, etc., etc.) and any number of respects in which he differs from them (he likes pistachio ice cream but they do not, etc., etc.). The crucial question is whether the compared objects resemble (and differ from) one another in *relevant* respects, that is, respects that are relevant to possession of the inferred resemblance. An argument by analogy based on resemblance in a few relevant respects is a "better" argument than one based on many irrelevant positive analogies.

The form of argument by analogy may now be *revised* as follows:

        (i)   *x* has characteristics F, G . . .
        (ii)  *y* has characteristics F, G . . .
        (iii) *x* also has characteristic H.
        (iv) <u>F, G . . . are H-relevant characteristics.</u>
        (v)  Therefore, *y* has characteristic H.

It seems fairly certain that in the kinds of examples we have been considering, a characteristic is "H-relevant" insofar as it is *causally* related to H, even if indirectly. (Brown's getting recommendations from his coaches shows, presumably, that he has an impressive personality, to the extent that sales prospects probably will buy cars from him.) But the relevance of one characteristic (F, say) to the possession of another characteristic (H, say) is not necessarily restricted to cases in which there is a causal connection between the former and the latter. Instead, F could be a criterion, or a member of a set of criteria, for possession of H, and thus be "H-relevant" in a *criterial* respect. The clarity with which a term paper is written, for instance, is one of a set of criteria for determining the grade it ought to receive. (These criteria do not have to be equal in weight—which is a point that raises complications that cannot be considered here.) This is hardly surprising, for the conclusion that a term paper deserves some particular grade is a *normative* conclusion. One can imagine using one term paper as a model for determining what the grade on some other term paper should be. In effect, one would be making an argument by analogy. Obviously, only grade-relevant characteristics should be taken into account in looking for the positive and negative analogies.[7]

Let us now turn to an example of a legal use of argument by analogy. Again, fuller discussion is postponed until the next chapter because of the role analogy often seems to play in appeals to precedent. But treatment here will enable an important problem concerning legal reasoning to be raised.

In *Adams v. New Jersey Steamboat Co.*,[8] it was held that where money for traveling expenses, carried by a passenger on a steamboat, was stolen from his stateroom at night, without negligence on his part, the carrier was liable therefore, without proof of negligence. Judge O'Brien argued by analogy from the liability of innkeepers. In his opinion he called a steamboat a "floating inn."

### ADAMS v. NEW JERSEY STEAMBOAT CO. (1896)

. . . The principle upon which innkeepers are charged by the common law as insurer of the money or personal effects of their guests originated in public policy. It was deemed to be a sound and necessary rule that this class of persons should be subjected to a high degree of responsibility in cases where an extraor-

---

[7] It should be noted that a characteristic might on occasion have a criterial relationship to the possession of some other characteristic because of a causal relationship holding between characteristics of the compared objects.

[8] 151 N.Y. 163, 45 N.E. 369

dinary confidence is necessarily reposed in them, and where great temptation to fraud and danger of plunder exists by reason of the peculiar relations of the parties. [Citation.] The relations that exist between a steamboat company and its passengers, who have procured staterooms for their comfort during the journey, differ in no essential respect from those that exist between the innkeeper and his guests. The passenger procures and pays for his room for the same reasons that a guest at an inn does. There are the same opportunities for fraud and plunder on the part of the carrier that was originally supposed to furnish a temptation to the landlord to violate his duty to the guest. A steamer carrying passengers upon the water, and furnishing them with rooms and entertainment is, for all practical purposes, a floating inn, and hence the duties which the proprietors owe to their charge ought to be the same. No good reason is apparent for relaxing the rigid rule of the common law which applies as between innkeeper and guest since the same considerations of public policy apply to both relations. . . .

. . . The two relations, if not identical, bear such close analogy to each other that the same rule of responsibility should govern. We are of the opinion, therefore, that the defendant was properly held liable in this case for the money stolen from the plaintiff, without any proof of negligence.

In basic outline, Judge O'Brien's argument fits the pattern of the revised form of argument by analogy. A possible brief formulation is this: (i) A hotel guest procures a room for personal use, and his money and personal effects are highly subject to fraud and plunder from the proprietor. (ii) A steamboat passenger procures a room for personal use, and his money and personal effects are highly subject to fraud and plunder from the proprietor. (iii) A hotel guest's proprietor has a stringent responsibility, such that the proprietor is liable, without proof of negligence, if money is stolen from the guest's room. (iv) Procuring a room for personal use and having one's money and personal effects highly subject to fraud and plunder from one's proprietor are reasons for the proprietor's having such a stringent responsibility. (v) Therefore, a steamboat passenger's proprietor is liable, without proof of negligence, if money is stolen from the passenger's room.

Premise (iv) states that the two mentioned characteristics are, as it were, "*H*-relevant," that is, grounds for imposing this degree of liability on certain proprietors (innkeepers and steamboat companies). But Judge O'Brien has also added another important point, namely, that considerations of "public policy" are the origin of the liability of innkeepers. This means, presumably, that the liability is imposed by the law in order to afford protection to members of the public who are in these special circumstances. The innkeeper rule on which O'Brien relies rests on an "appeal to public policy" and, in a sense, so does his argument. "Appeal to public policy," is an often-used catch-all *kind of reason* for accepting some proposition as a rule of law, though the reason can be made fairly specific in this case. The conclusion of the argument is of course normative. But the two characteristics do not function in the argument as direct criterial considerations for the imposition of liability, in the way that grade-relevant considerations do for meriting a particular grade. Rather, the characteristics appear to be components of a kind of *goal-oriented* justification for imposing the liability, the goal being the protection of a segment of the community that is especially vulnerable to theft.

We shall come back to *Adams v. New Jersey Steamboat Co.* and other examples of analogical argument later. Meanwhile, we are now in a position to raise an important problem.

The discussion of form began with deductive arguments. A deductive argument purports that its premises are sufficient to establish the truth of its conclusion, and this will be the case if all the premises are true and the argument is formally valid (an instance of a valid argument form). Judges of course give formally valid deductive arguments, as we saw in *Lubitz v. Wells*. But they also give arguments that in terms of logical structure have the form of nondeductive arguments, as we saw in the *Steamboat* case. Now, it is a feature of nondeductive arguments that their form is not sufficient to establish the truth of their conclusions even if all their premises are true, as was noted in the discussion of nonnormative arguments. Such arguments at best show only that the conclusions are more likely to be true than false.

But would this be an appropriate characterization of Judge O'Brien's argument? Although his argument has the form of a nondeductive argument, he apparently presumes to have established the truth (or correctness), rather than the mere likelihood, of his conclusion on the basis of the premises he uses. And, it would seem, so do other judges make this presumption when they employ arguments by analogy. The problem is whether this presumption is well founded. In the next chapter it is suggested that this presumption—that legal arguments by analogy can be sufficient to establish the truth or correctness of their conclusions—is connected with the fact that these arguments are normative in character. But this is only part of the story. Meanwhile, we can say that a judicial argument by analogy that has all true (or correct) premises establishes its conclusion as highly plausible.

A brief summary of the highlights of the discussion in this chapter might be useful at this point. (1) The discussion began with the statement that judicial arguments can be viewed from two perspectives: the logical form of the arguments and the kinds of reasons given for a conclusion (e.g., "appeal to good sense"). (2) From the perspective of form, two sorts of arguments were distinguished, deductive and nondeductive. (3) In a deductive argument, the premises purport to be sufficient to establish the conclusion as true. A "good" deductive argument is one that is formally valid (an instance of a valid argument form) and all of whose premises are true. (4) In a nondeductive argument, the premises purport to establish the conclusion as more likely to be true than false. A nondeductive argument is not formally valid; the truth of the premises does not entail the truth of the conclusion. (5) The conclusions of judicial arguments are normative rather than descriptive; these conclusions in effect amount to a claim as to how a case or class of cases ought to be decided. (6) Some judicial arguments are, or can be formulated as, deductive arguments. (7) Judicial arguments by analogy, however, have the form of nondeductive arguments. These judicial arguments are problematic since they seem to be intended as sufficient to establish their conclusions as true (or correct). (8) In analogical arguments the strength of the argument depends, in part, on the relevance of the premises to the conclusion (the relevance of the assumed resemblances to the inferred resemblance).

## Kinds of Reasons

In the course of exposition of the above points, reference was occasionally made to the *kinds of reasons* used by judges. It is now time to begin the transition to this subject. This will be done by analyzing a judicial opinion in some detail, employing some of the concepts derived from the discussion of argument forms. Here is a case from the North Carolina Supreme Court.

### JOYNER v. JOYNER (1862)[9]

Petition for divorce. . . . The petitioner alleged her marriage with the defendant; that she herself was well-bred and of respectable family, and that her husband was not less than a fair match for her; that her husband had struck her with a horse-whip on one occasion, and with a switch on another, leaving several bruises on her person; and that on several occasions he had used abusive and insulting language towards her. The petition concluded as set forth in the opinion of court.

CHIEF JUSTICE PEARSON:

The legislature has deemed it expedient to enlarge the grounds upon which divorces may be obtained; but as check or restraint on applications for divorces,

---

[9] 59 N.C. 322 (1862). Note that the court is not deciding whether Mrs. Joyner should be granted a divorce but only the question of law presented below.

and to guard against abuses, it is provided that the cause or ground on which the divorce is asked for shall be set forth in the petition "particularly and specially. . . ."

. . .[We] are of opinion that it was necessary to state the circumstances under which the blow with the horse-whip, and the blows with the switch, were given; for instance, what was the conduct of the petitioner; what had she done, or said, to induce such violence on the part of the husband? We are informed by the petitioner that she was a woman, "well-bred, and of respectable family, and that her husband was not less than a fair match for her." There is no allegation that he was drunk, nor was there any imputation of unfaithfulness on either side (which is the most common ingredient of applications for divorce), so there was an obvious necessity for some explanation, and the cause of divorce could not be set forth, "particularly and specially," without stating the circumstances which gave rise to the alleged grievances.

It was said on the argument that the fact that a husband on one occasion "struck his wife with a horse-whip, and on another occasion with a switch, leaving several bruises on her person," is of itself a sufficient cause of divorce, and consequently the circumstances which attended the infliction of these injuries are immaterial, and need not be set forth. This presents the question in the case.

The wife must be subject to the husband. Every man must govern his household, and if by reason of an unruly temper, or an unbridled tongue, the wife persistently treats her husband with disrespect, and he submits to it, he not only loses all sense of self-respect, but loses the respect of the other members of his family, without which he cannot expect to govern them, and forfeits the respect of his neighbors. Such have been the incidents of the marriage relation from the beginning of the human race. Unto the woman it is said: "Thy desire shall be to thy husband, and he shall rule over thee": Gen. iii. 16. It follows that the law gives the husband power to use such a degree of force as necessary to make the wife behave herself and know her place. . . .

[The] law gives this power to the husband over the person of the wife, and has adopted proper safeguards to prevent an abuse of it.

We will not pursue the discussion further. It is not an agreeable subject, and we are not inclined unnecessarily to draw upon ourselves the charge of a want of proper respect for the weaker sex. It is sufficient for our purpose to state that there may be circumstances which will mitigate, excuse, and so far justify the husband in striking the wife "with a horse-whip on one occasion and with a switch on another, leaving several bruises on the person," so as not to give her a right to abandon him, and claim to be divorced. For instance, suppose a husband comes home, and his wife abuses him in the strongest terms—calls him a scoundrel, and repeatedly expresses a wish that he was dead and in torment; and being thus provoked in furor brevis, he strikes her with the horse-whip, which he happens to have in his hands, but is afterwards willing to apologize, and expresses regret for having struck her; or suppose a man and his wife get into a discussion and have a difference of opinion as to a matter of fact, she becomes furious and gives way to her temper, so far as to tell him he lies, and upon being admonished not to repeat the word, nevertheless does so, and the husband taking up a switch, tells her if she repeats it again he will strike her, and after this notice she again repeats the insulting words, and he thereupon strikes her several blows,—these are cases in which, in our opinion, the circumstances attending the act, and giving rise to it, so far justify the conduct of the husband as to take from the wife any ground of divorce for that cause, and authorize the court to dismiss her petition, with the admonition, "If you will amend your manners, you may expect better treatment": See Shelford on Divorce. So that there are circumstances under which a husband may strike his wife with a horse-whip, or may strike her several times with a switch, so hard as to leave marks on her person, and these acts do not furnish sufficient ground for a divorce. It follows that when such acts are alleged as the causes for a divorce, it is necessary in order to comply with the provisions of the statute to state the circumstances attending the acts, and which gave rise to them. . . .

In approaching the analysis of Chief Justice Pearson's opinion, it is very important, first, to see clearly the question of law he is ruling on. Second, it is helpful to have in mind the main conclusion in the case. To some extent Pearson is concerned with the interpretation of a statute. The divorce statute provides (to guard against abuses) that a petition for divorce must state the ground on which divorce is sought, and that this ground must be set forth "particularly and specially." The question before Pearson, then, is whether or not the provisions of the statute are satisfied by a wife's petition that merely alleges that "her husband had struck her with a horse-whip on one occasion, and a switch on another, leaving several bruises on her person." The petitioner (Mrs. Joyner) claims that this fact is itself sufficient grounds for divorce; and Chief Justice Pearson seems to agree that if this is correct, the petition would satisfy the provisions of the statute without having to state the circumstances that attended infliction of the injuries. Pearson's answer to the question of law is given in the last sentence of the opinion, namely, that "it is necessary in order to comply with the provisions of the statute to state the circumstances attending the acts [of wife-beating], and which gave rise to them," which is the main conclusion.

Pearson's main argument, moreover, is encapsulated in the last two sentences of the opinion. Let us formulate the argument, making explicit its premises and conclusion:

(i)  If there are circumstances in which a husband is justified in striking his wife with a horse-whip, etc., then being struck with a horse-whip, etc., is itself not sufficient grounds for divorce.

(ii)  <u>If</u> being struck with a horse-whip, etc., is itself not sufficient grounds for divorce, <u>then</u> it is necessary, in order to comply with the statute, to state the circumstances attending the acts.

(iii) There are circumstances in which a husband is justified in striking his wife with a horse-whip, etc.

(iv) Therefore, it is necessary, in order to comply with the statute, to state the circumstances attending the acts.

This argument clearly is a *valid* argument, as can easily be seen if letters are used to stand for sentences. Let

*A* stand for "There are circumstances in which a husband is justified in striking his wife, etc.";

*B* stand for "Being struck with a horse-whip, etc., is itself not sufficient ground for divorce"; and

*C* stand for "It is necessary, in order to comply with the statute, to state the circumstances attending the acts."

The argument will now be seen to have the form

(i′)   <u>If</u> *A*, <u>then</u> *B*.
(ii′)  <u>If</u> *B*, <u>then</u> *C*.
(iii′) *A*
(iv′)  Therefore, *C*.

Any argument of this form, in which *A*, *B*, and *C* are appropriately and uniformly substituted for by sentences, is a *valid* argument.

But is Pearson's argument *sound*? This turns us to the question of whether all the premises of the argument are true (or correct).

Pearson's argument rests on a certain assumption that is more or less explicit in his opinion. This assumption (*T*) states the following proposition of law:

(*T*) Being struck with a horse-whip, etc., is itself sufficient grounds for divorce <u>only if</u> there never are circumstances in which a husband is justified <u>in</u> striking his wife with a horse-whip, etc.

Or put in simpler terms, wife-beating is sufficient grounds for divorce only if a husband never is justified in beating his wife. Pearson assumes that (*T*) is a correct statement of the law, and premise (i) results from (*T*) by a simple transposition;[10] so premise (i) is a correct statement of the law. Now it should be obvious that the legislature could have explicitly made wife-beating itself a sufficient ground for divorce, but apparently it had not. In any event, premise (i), and the other premises as well, should be understood as having attached to them some such qualifier as ''under North Carolina law in 1862.'' (In a more technical account of judicial argument, this sort of qualifier may pose a problem; but it is unnecessary to discuss it here.) Premise (ii) seems to be correct also, as a reading of the requirements of the divorce statute.

Before turning to premise (iii) it should be noted that the considerations of the above paragraph, though Chief Justice Pearson does not spell them out, fairly may be taken to represent Pearson's *reasons* for regarding premises (i) and (ii) as true or correct. If one thinks of the main argument of an opinion as consisting of the premises leading to the result in a case, then one may view the question of the *kinds of reasons* a judge has for the conclusion as concerned with why a judge thinks he is *justified* in accepting the premises as true or correct. (Since a case can pose more than one question of law, it may have more than one result and, so to speak, more than one main argument.) Plainly, if a judge is justified in accepting all the premises and if the conclusion, the result, follows logically from the premises, then he is also justified in accepting the conclusion as correct—unless the legal system is anomalous. In Pearson's case, his reason for thinking himself justified in accepting premises (i) and (ii) is not much more than that they each represent the law of the state of North Carolina, although it sounds somewhat redundant to put it in this way. More specifically, he regards each of these premises as following from a principle of North Carolina law or as implicit in one of its statutes. One may call Pearson's kind of reason an ''appeal to the law.''

A moment ago it was stated that one may view the question of kinds of reasons as concerned with a judge's justification for accepting a premise. Very often a judge will make his justification explicit and will offer an argument for the premise. This can be called a subsidiary argument. Frequently, however, a judge will run together the main and subsidiary arguments, and

---

[10] Where P and Q stand for sentences, from

    If P, then Q (or P only if Q)

it may be inferred that

    If it is not the case that Q, then it is not the case that P.

it will be difficult to disentangle a premise in the main argument from the reason given for accepting the premise—for a premise after all is also one of the reasons for the conclusion. So the distinction between a premise and the kind of reason a judge has for accepting a premise may be somewhat artificial in some contexts. Nevertheless, the distinction is a useful analytical tool for understanding judicial argument and legal reasoning. Naturally, a judge may have more than one kind of reason for a premise or have different kinds of reasons for accepting different premises. In these instances, it is a combination of kinds of reasons that leads to the conclusion.

But a qualification should be added here. We saw in *Lubitz v. Wells* that Judge Troland offers a reason for *rejecting* a certain proposition (that the golf club is "so obviously and intrinsically [a] dangerous [object]") as a true or correct statement. His reason is an appeal to "good sense." The question of the kind of reason, therefore, must be understood as being as much concerned with why a judge thinks himself justified in rejecting some statement as it is concerned with the acceptance of a premise. However, this qualification will not be explicitly mentioned in the rest of the discussion.

To return to *Joyner v. Joyner*, the problematic premise in Pearson's argument is (iii). Is it true (or correct) that there are circumstances in which a husband is justified in striking his wife with a horse-whip so as to leave bruises on her person? Is wife-beating ever justified? The subsidiary argument of *Joyner v. Joyner* is directed toward establishing premise (iii). Most of the opinion, in fact, deals with this issue. The subsidiary argument starts with the paragraph that begins "The wife must be subject to the husband," and it ends just before the last two sentences of the opinion. Here, a very different sort of reason from the kind identified earlier seems to be operative.

This argument moves in three stages. In the first, Chief Justice Pearson presents a certain conception of the family, from which he draws a particular conclusion of law. Second, in a portion omitted from the excerpt, he maintains that this conclusion is reflected in other principles of the law. And third, he applies the conclusion to the facts of the *Joyner* case, thereby justifying his acceptance of premise (iii). The first stage obviously is the most crucial: it is the conception of the family as a social institution in which the husband is the governing authority that leads to the conclusion of law that the husband should have the legal power (the right) to use such force as is necessary to make the wife behave herself. Recognition of this power is shown in other principles of the common law, but the power can be abused. Still, Pearson argues, situations can be imagined in which even such a degree of force as in the *Joyner* case could be appropriate.

## Practical Reasoning[11]

But why should this conception of the family (or any other conception of the family, for that matter) lead to a conclusion of *law*, a conclusion about the *legal* rights of the husband? Pearson plainly is assuming that preservation of the family—with the structure he regards as being inherent to it—is a *goal* that the law ought to promote, and therefore that legal recognition should be given to the *means* that are necessary to achieve this goal (a right to use force). In general terms, this is a "goal-oriented" kind of reason, and it is quite different from an appeal to the law, which was Pearson's reason for accepting premises (i) and (ii). Pearson, in effect, is engaging here in a particular type of *practical reasoning*:

(A)  *X* is a goal the law ought to promote.
(B)  *Y* is a necessary means to *X*.
(C)  Therefore, *Y* ought to be recognized by the law.

The explanation of why this argument is called "practical" is that implicit in the major (A) premise is the idea that something should be *done* to bring about the envisioned circumstance. Practical reasoning supplies an appropriately situated person with a *reason for* taking action, which is also a feature of norms, generally. Given (A) and the statement about means, a specific action is mandated, which is expressed in the "ought" of the conclusion. The conclusion supplies such a person with a reason for doing a specific thing. In the case of courts, these doings consist of rendering certain judgments, according or acknowledging certain rights.

In relation to *Joyner,* in which *X* in the practical syllogism stands for the preservation of the family and *Y* for a husband's right to use force, the conclusion supplies Justice Pearson with a reason for according or acknowledging such a right. Applying this right to the circumstances of the case, Pearson regards premise (iii) as justified. Obviously, though, it is the premise about family preservation that is crucial. This goal-oriented reason has a much wider sphere of applicability than any direct appeal to the law of the state of North Carolina in 1862. If it is a *good reason* it ought to be attractive to judges in other jurisdictions, too.

[11] On this general subject, advanced students may wish to consult Joseph Raz (ed.), *Practical Reasoning* (Oxford: Oxford University Press, 1978) and Joseph Raz, *Practical Reason and Norms* (London: Hutchinson University Library, 1975).

Is it a good reason? This question raises difficult problems in the philosophy of law, ethics, and political philosophy, and it can be dealt with only in outline. Let us proceed step by step.

One of the important criteria for something to be a good reason is that it must be true (or correct or acceptable). Now in Chief Justice Pearson's main argument, which was laid out a few pages earlier, premises (i) and (ii) were regarded as true or correct because they were justified by an appeal to existing laws of the state. This point can be generalized: some, at least, of the legal assertions made by judges are to be regarded as true or correct if and only if they are justifiable by reference to the *authoritative sources* of the law (of the given system). Included in these authoritative sources are constitutions, codes, statutes, and, in Anglo-American law, precedents (decisions in prior cases). The general problem of how the authoritative sources are to be identified is a much debated topic in the philosophy of law. Students of legal philosophy will recognize this as part of the problem of legal "validity."[12]

In regard to Pearson's practical argument, the issue of truth or correctness is more complicated. Consider the following argument—which is another variety of practical reasoning, although the word "ought" does not appear in the major premise:

(a) Preservation of the family is a good.
(b) A husband's right to use force to make his wife behave herself is a necessary means to this good.
(c) Therefore, such a right ought to be recognized.

Taken as it is, this goal-oriented practical argument is not a legal practical argument: it says nothing about the law. Instead, it is a moral or ethical argument, and its conclusion is about the recognition of a moral right. Again, however, if (a) is to be regarded as a good reason, the question of its truth (or correctness) arises. Is preservation of the family a good? And assuming this to be the case, is the governance of the family by the husband inherent to the structure of the family? For instance, is it true that the family, like certain other social institutions, needs a locus of final authority, and if it does, should that authority reside in the husband? These last questions are in part descriptive questions, to which the data of the social and behavioral

---

[12] For prominent modern treatments, see Hans Kelsen, *General Theory of Law and State* (Cambridge, Mass: Harvard University Press, 1945), and H. L. A. Hart, *The Concept of Law* (Oxford: Oxford University Press, 1961); see also John Chipman Gray, *The Nature and Sources of the Law* (Boston: Beacon Press, 1963; first published 1909).

sciences are relevant. But they are not purely descriptive questions. For the issue of family governance is one that concerns the function of the family and the contribution it should make toward promoting the well-being of its members. These questions, then, are in part also ethical, and in order to answer them one needs a theory of the good life and a theory of human nature.

Assuming, for the sake of discussion, that premise (a) can be established as true or correct from an ethical perspective, so that one has a good reason for doing something to bring about the goal, it is important to note that it is not necessarily the case that every good moral reason for doing something is also a good *legal* reason for doing something, and vice versa. A full treatment of this rather dogmatically asserted proposition, with all the required qualifications, would take us too far afield. The following considerations, however, may be briefly pleaded in defense of it: first, that one is morally obligated to do many things that one is not legally obligated to do; and second, that legal systems differ from one another in content. This second consideration also shows an important feature about law. It shows that a legal assertion that is true (or correct) in one legal system need not necessarily be true (or correct) in another legal system. Furthermore, it shows that a good legal reason in one system need not be a good legal reason in another system.

Let us suppose that Chief Justice Pearson implicitly uses the above practical moral argument in *Joyner*. In order for (a) to be a good *legal* reason for Pearson, (a) would have to be true in the legal system in which he is operating. In effect, then, the issue would be whether preservation of the family *is* a goal the system ought to promote. But this is equivalent to asking whether (A), in the original practical argument, is true in that legal system.

Now, it would seem to be the case that when a person assumes a judicial role in any system, he or she assumes a duty to decide cases in accord with the laws of the system. Most often, when a question of law arises for the judge, he or she appropriately will decide the question by reference to the authoritative sources of law for that system. But in some cases (as in *Joyner*) the judge will appropriately decide questions of law also by reference to the *ends* or *goals* that the system is presumed to have. (Chief Justice Pearson can hardly be supposed to have thought that he was going outside of the existing law of North Carolina or that he was expressing a personal moral judgment, in tying his argument to the goal of family preservation. Undoubtedly, he thought that this goal was implicit in the legislation governing divorces, and that he was "finding" or "declaring," rather than "making," the law on the issue before his court.) The truth or correctness of statements such as (A) presupposes the existence of such goals. The promotion of these goals is also part of the judge's duty. It is not claimed, of course, that it is always clear what these goals are or that they are never controversial. In any event, it is in relationship to such presumed goals that one determines the truth or correctness of the major premises of practical legal arguments of the sort considered here.

But there is a further point. Two paragraphs ago it was supposed that Chief Justice Pearson implicitly employed the mentioned practical moral argument. But this is not mere supposition, for Pearson's argument sounds suspiciously like a moral argument. This is not surprising. For although there is a distinction between good moral reasons and good legal reasons, there has never been a clear-cut separation between them in Anglo-American judicial practice. When important social or institutional goals and interests have been at stake, judges have very often assumed that such presumably ethically justifiable goals are goals that the legal system should promote. Thus the *value judgments* judges use or make, explicitly or implicitly, play a vital role in their reasoning. It is clear, I think, that in order to establish the truth or correctness of premise (iii), Pearson had to use or make a series of value judgments.

The question, then, whether Pearson's goal-oriented reason is a good reason implicates a host of ethical complexities, and this is true of other goal-oriented reasons offered by judges. A number of such reasons are identified in an article by Professor Robert S. Summers.[13] Among them are general safety, community welfare, facilitation of democracy, and public health. All of these goals involve the courts with value judgments and the type of practical reasoning mentioned earlier or its variants. One of these variants is "negative." It runs something like this:

*X* is a goal the law ought to promote.
*Y* impedes, or would impede, the realization of *X*.
Therefore, *Y* ought to be prevented by the law.

Another instance is:

*X* is a goal the law ought to promote.
Legal recognition of *Y* would defeat the realization of *X*.
Therefore, *Y* ought not to be legally recognized.

---

[13] Robert S. Summers, "Two Types of Substantive Reasons: The Core of a Theory of Common-Law Justification," *Cornell Law Review*, 63 (1978), pp. 707-788.

Both of these examples are forms of practical *reductio ad absurdum* argument, which was mentioned at the beginning of this chapter. They often are employed, explicitly or implicitly, in judicial opinions that give goal-oriented reasons.

This part of the discussion concludes with the brief introduction of two important qualifications of the original formulation of practical reasoning. Let us assume that some particular $X$ is a goal the law ought to promote. It could be the case that there is more than one way to accomplish this end; either $Y$ or $Z$ could do the job. In such a situation, neither $Y$ nor $Z$ would be a necessary means to $X$. So a judge might well decide to give legal recognition to both $Y$ and $Z$, or he or she might decide to recognize the one that constituted the "best" means to $X$. But, more important, even if $Y$ were a necessary means to $X$, there might be considerations that militated against according legal recognition to $Y$; recognition of $Y$ might defeat $W$, another goal or good end that the law ought to promote. Thus there would be a good reason for giving legal recognition to $Y$ and a good reason for not giving legal recognition to $Y$. The original "syllogism" of legal practical reasoning should be reformulated as follows:

(A')   $X$ is a goal the law ought to promote.
(B')   $Y$ is a necessary means to $X$.
(C')   Therefore, if there are no countervailing
        considerations, $Y$ ought to be recognized
        by the law.

(A more complicated reformulation will be needed for cases in which there is more than one way to achieve the goal.) Where there are countervailing considerations, one may have two practical arguments, positive and negative, which lead to seemingly opposite results. Presumably, the rider "if there are no countervailing considerations" should be read into the practical argument implicit in Chief Justice Pearson's opinion. When countervailing considerations exist in a case, the judge will have to decide in accordance with the relative "weights" of the considerations.

At this point, it would be appropriate to treat the topic of *coherence*. For not only are judges expected to render decisions that are coherent with the existing law and the goals of the system, but it is also assumed that the system's laws and goals are internally coherent on the whole. It can be plausibily argued that there are respects in which our legal system is not internally coherent. But it is extremely difficult to spell out what "coherence" means, and this subject will be bypassed.[14] It may be mentioned, however, that the next section bears on the issue.

These remarks conclude the analysis of *Joyner v. Joyner.* We have seen some of the elements that go into judicial argument and have examined the opinion from the perspective of the logical form of the argument and the kinds of reasons used by judges. Although the opinion in *Joyner* is rather straightforward as compared with many other opinions, detailed analysis has shown how complex the elements of a judicial argument can be and how they may give rise to difficult questions of ethics and of political and legal philosophy. Judges of course employ arguments having forms different from the one in *Joyner*, and they also use reasons that are different in kind from Pearson's appeals to the law and the (goal-oriented) appeal to preservation of the family. Although rules can be given for generating all the logical forms of arguments that judges may employ, there is no official finite list of the specific kinds of reasons to which judges appeal. All one can do is study many judicial arguments and see whether there are certain broad categories into which the various reasons fall.

## Conflicting Decisions

In the remainder of this chapter we shall look at two cases that represent an interesting phenomenon in the law, the understanding of which is important to the field of legal reasoning: on substantially the same set of facts, two courts may reach opposite results. These cases tell us a great deal about how judges conceive the nature of the judicial role. In each case the plaintiff's picture was used, without permission, to advertise a product. The question is whether or not there is a "right of privacy," which when violated gives rise to a cause of action. It is acknowledged that the courts are being asked to do something new, namely, to recognize a right that hitherto had not been accorded explicit legal recognition. The New York court (1902) refuses to take this forward step, whereas the Georgia court (1904) does. The opinions will

---

[14] Advanced students may wish to consult the following works, which have discussions relevant to this point: Neil MacCormick, *Legal Reasoning and Legal Theory* (Oxford: Clarendon Press, 1978); Rolf Sartorius, *Individual Conduct and Social Norms* (Encino, Calif.: Dickenson Publishing Co., 1975, chap. 10; and two stimulating but difficult chapters, *"The Model of Rules II"* and *"Hard Cases"* in Ronald Dworkin, *Taking Rights Seriously* (Cambridge, Mass. Harvard University Press, 1978). The view of judicial reasoning presented by Dworkin runs counter to the treatment presented thus far in the text. Dworkin negates the role of "arguments of policy," which goal-oriented practical arguments are, in effect.

not be analyzed in the same detail as before. The focus of attention will be on the kinds of reasons the judges use; less attention will be given to the form of the arguments.

The New York case was decided by a majority of 4 to 3. Here are excerpts from the majority opinion, written by Chief Judge Parker, who states the facts of the case.

## ROBERSON v. ROCHESTER FOLDING BOX CO. (1902)[15]

The complaint alleges that the Franklin Mills Co., one of the defendants, was engaged in a general milling business and in the manufacture and sale of flour; that before the commencement of the action without the knowledge or consent of plaintiff, defendants, knowing that they had no right or authority so to do, had obtained, made, printed, sold and circulated about 25,000 lithographic prints, photographs and likenesses of plaintiff, made in a manner particularly set up in the complaint; that upon the paper upon which the likenesses were printed and above the portrait there were printed, in large, plain letters, the words, "Flour of the Family," and below the portrait in large capital letters, "Franklin Mills Flour," and in the lower right-hand corner in smaller capital letters "Rochester Folding Box Co., Rochester, N.Y.;" that upon the same sheet were other advertisements of the flour of the Franklin Mills Co.; that those 25,000 likenesses of the plaintiff thus ornamented have been conspicuously posted and displayed in stores, warehouses, saloons and other public places; that they have been recognized by friends of the plaintiff and other people with the result that plaintiff has been greatly humiliated by the scoffs and jeers of persons who have recognized her face and picture on this advertisement and her good name has been attacked, causing her great distress and suffering both in body and mind; that she was made sick and suffered a severe nervous shock, was confined to her bed and compelled to employ a physician, because of these facts; that defendants had continued to print, make, use, sell and circulate the said lithographs, and that by reason of the foregoing facts plaintiff had suffered damages in the sum of $15,000. The complaint prays that defendants be enjoined from making, printing, publishing, circulating or using in any manner any likenesses of plaintiff in any form whatever, for further relief (which it is not necessary to consider here) and for damages.

It will be observed that there is no complaint made that plaintiff was libeled by this publication of her portrait. The likeness is said to be a very good one, and one that her friends and acquaintances were able to recognize; indeed, her grievance is that a good portrait of her, and, therefore one easily recognized, has been used to attract attention toward the paper upon which defendant mill company's advertisements appear. Such publicity, which some find agreeable, is to plaintiff very

[15] 171 N.Y. 538 (1902).

distasteful, and thus, because of defendants' impertinence in using her picture without her consent for their own business purposes, she has been caused to suffer mental distress where others would have appreciated the compliment to their beauty implied in the selection of the picture for such purposes; but as it is distasteful to her, she seeks the aid of the courts to enjoin a further circulation of the lithographic prints containing her portrait made as alleged in the complaint, and as an incident thereto, to reimburse her for the damages to her feelings, which the complaint fixes at the sum of $15,000.

There is no precedent for such an action to be found in the decisions of this court. . . . Mention of such a right is not to be found in Blackstone, Kent or any other of the great commentators upon the law, nor so far as the learning of counsel or the courts in this case have been able to discover, does its existence seem to have been asserted prior to about the year 1890, when it was presented with attractiveness and no inconsiderable ability in the Harvard Law Review (Vol. IV, page 193) in an article entitled "The Right of [sic] Privacy."[16]

The so-called right of privacy is, as the phrase suggests, founded upon the claim that a man has the right to pass through this world, if he wills, without having his picture published, his business enterprises discussed, his successful experiments written up for the benefit of others, or his eccentricities commented upon either in handbills, circulars, catalogues, periodicals or newspapers, and, necessarily, that the things which may not be written and published of him must not be spoken of him by his neighbors, whether the comment be favorable or otherwise. While most persons would much prefer to have a good likeness of themselves appear in a responsible periodical or leading newspaper rather than upon an advertising card or sheet, the doctrine which the courts are asked to create for this case would apply as well to the one publication as to the other, for the principle which a court of equity is asked to assert in support of a recovery in this action is that the right of privacy exists and is enforceable in equity, and that the publication of that which purports to be a portrait of another person, even if obtained upon the street by an impertinent individual with a camera, will be restrained in equity on the ground that an individual has the right to prevent his features from becoming known to those outside of his circle of friends and acquaintances.

If such a principle be incorporated into the body of the law through the instrumentality of a court of equity,[17] the attempts to logically apply the principle will necessarily result, not only in a vast amount of litigation, but in litigation bordering upon the absurd, for the right of privacy, once established as a legal doctrine, cannot be confined to the restraint of the publication of a likeness but must necessarily embrace as well the publication of a word-picture, a comment

---

[16] An excerpt from this article, by Samuel D. Warren and Louis D. Brandeis (the future U.S. Supreme Court justice), is contained in the materials for this chapter.

[17] *Equity* is the administration of justice based on principles of fairness instead of on strict rules of common law.

upon one's looks, conduct, domestic relations or habits. And were the right of privacy once legally asserted, it would necessarily be held to include the same things if spoken instead of printed, for one, as well as the other, invades the right to be absolutely let alone. An insult would certainly be in violation of such a right and with many persons would more seriously wound the feelings than would the publication of their picture. . . .

The legislative body could very well interfere and arbitrarily provide that no one should be permitted for his own selfish purpose to use the picture or the name of another for advertising purposes without his consent. In such event, no embarrassment would result to the general body of the law, for the rule would be applicable only to cases provided for by the statute. The courts, however, being without authority to legislate, are required to decide cases upon principle, and so are necessarily embarrassed by precedents created by an extreme, and, therefore, unjustifiable application of an old principle. . . .

[Parker reviews the cases cited in the *Harvard Law Review* article.]

In not one of these cases, therefore, was it the basis of the decision that the defendant could be restrained from performing the act he was doing or threatening to do on the ground that the feelings of the plaintiff would be thereby injured; but, on the contrary, each decision was rested either upon the ground of breach of trust or that plaintiff has a property right in the subject of litigation, which the court could protect. . . .

[Parker reviews some more recent cases.]

An examination of the authorities leads us to the conclusion that the so-called "right of privacy" has not as yet found an abiding place in our jurisprudence, and, as we view it, the doctrine cannot now be incorporated without doing violence to settled principles of law by which the profession and the public have long been guided. . . .

It is left to the reader, as an exercise, to identify the premises employed by Judge Parker and to sketch out the argument's overall form. We can begin our analysis by noting that *Roberson* is illustrative of argumentation against a change in the law or the introduction of a new legal principle. Parker uses a variety of practical *reductio ad absurdum* argument when he states that the recognition of a right of privacy would lead to litigation "bordering on the absurd." But why is this so? The most important part of the opinion for our purposes concerns the judge's statements about the difference between the ways in which a court and a legislature may handle cases of this kind.

A legislature may enact a finely drawn law that would accord relief to an aggrieved party in just those circumstances complained of by Roberson. (The New York State legislature in fact did so soon after the decision.) A court, however, says Judge Parker, must decide cases "on principle." This means that the reason, or main ground, on which the result is based must have a *generality* of application that goes beyond the particular case being ruled on and sometimes also beyond the kind of case being decided. A judicial decision may not be *ad hoc*, that is, grounded on the specific facts of the instant case; it must be subsumed under a general principle, so that the instant case is decided in a particular way because the judge regards it right to decide cases of its *kind* in that way. (Analogous to judicial decision, it is a requirement of scientific explanation that it be framed in terms broader than the particular occurrence that is being explained.)

The requirement that judges should decide cases "on principle" is related to the idea of *fairness*, which demands that like cases should be treated alike. The notion of decision " on principle," however, is somewhat broader than the idea of fairness; for principled decision requires that the instant case should be subsumed under a general reason, from which the decision follows for the instant case and all relevantly similar cases. Nevertheless, it is extremely difficult to lay down any exact criterion for the degree of generality that a principle should have. Moreover, it does not seem possible to formulate any rule for determining the relevant similarities among cases. In any event, when a judge thinks it proper to draw a distinction among cases that appear to him to be similar in relevant respects, it is required that the distinction be made in a principled fashion, that is, on a relevant general ground. Principled decision forbids the making of arbitrary distinctions, and its constraints promote judicial rationality and objectivity.

It is precisely his inability to draw a principled distinction among cases—he believes it is insufficient merely to say that *Roberson* is a "picture case"—that leads Judge Parker to reject Roberson's claim to have a cause of action. The alleged right of privacy on which Roberson bases her claim is an extremely general right. As Parker interprets it, this right would include not only the right not to have one's picture used without permission for commercial purposes, but also the right not to be insulted and the right not to be gossiped about. But Parker does not think that anyone has these latter rights. How, then, shall a principled distinction be drawn between those privacy rights that the law should recognize and those alleged privacy rights that it should not recognize? Since Parker, by self-admission, is unable to formulate such a distinction, he would have to acknowledge a general right of privacy in order to decide in favor of Roberson—but such a principle could not be delimited and would set a precedent that would "necessarily embarrass" later courts. It would be merely arbitrary to recognize only a right not to have one's picture used for commercial purposes. A legislature could do this but a court cannot, for judges are forbidden to legislate.

Although both Chief Judge Parker's opinion in *Roberson* and Chief

Justice Pearson's opinion in *Joyner* are concerned with rights, there is an important difference between the two. The issue in *Joyner* is whether a certain right (a husband's right to physically chastise his wife) should be legally recognized in order to promote a particular *goal*. The issue in *Roberson*, on the other hand, is whether a certain claimed right (a person's right not to have his or her picture used for commercial purposes) should be legally recognized because it falls under a more general legal *right*. Had the New York court recognized the claimed right, its reason for doing so would have been a "rights-oriented" kind of reason rather than a goal-oriented reason. As it turned out, the court refused this legal recognition because of a practical *reductio ad absurdum* argument, with regard to which one should distinguish a goal-oriented variety from a rights-oriented variety. Under the first variety, a court may refuse to recognize a certain claimed right because so doing would frustrate the realization of some particular goal or good end. Under the second variety, as in *Roberson*, a court may refuse to recognize a certain claimed right because so doing would require the recognition of other alleged rights that it maintains should not be recognized. Still, *Roberson* does utilize a goal-oriented practical *reductio ad absurdum*—to the extent that it is argued that legal recognition of a right of privacy would result in " a vast amount of litigation" and thus, presumably, impede the functioning of the courts.[18]

Just two years after *Roberson* was decided, the Supreme Court of Georgia was presented with a case involving a similar set of facts. It is rather fascinating that the Georgia court unanimously arrived at the opposite result. Here is an excerpt from Justice Cobb's opinion in *Pavesich v. New England Life Insurance Co.*, written for the court. Although lengthy, it is worth a careful reading. All aspects of this case cannot be examined here. But it, too, raises the issue of the nature of the judicial role.

## PAVESICH v. NEW ENGLAND LIFE INSURANCE CO. (1904)[19]

Paolo Pavesich brought an action against the New England Mutual Life Insurance Company, a non-resident corporation, Thomas B. Lumpkin, its general agent, and J. Q. Adams, a photographer, both residing in the city of Atlanta. The allegations of the petition were, in substance, as follows: In an issue of the *Atlanta Constitution*, a newspaper published in the city of Atlanta, there appeared a likeness of the plaintiff, which would be easily recognized by his friends and ac-

---

[18] In the article by Robert S. Summers mentioned earlier (p. 58), two types of substantive reasons are emphasized: "goal reasons" and "rightness reasons." What in this book is called a rights-oriented reason comes under the latter heading, which includes such items as punitive desert, justified reliance, restitution for unjust enrichment, and comparative blame.
[19] 122 Ga. 190 (1904).

quaintances, placed by the side of the likeness of an ill-dressed and sickly looking person. Above the likeness of the plaintiff were the words, "Do it now. The man who did." Above the likeness of the other person were the words, "Do it while you can. The man who didn't." Below the two pictures were the words, "These two pictures tell their own story." Under the plaintiff's picture the following appeared: "In my healthy and productive period of life I bought insurance in the New England Mutual Life Insurance Co., of Boston, Mass., and to-day my family is protected and I am drawing an annual dividend on my paid-up policies." Under the other person's picture was a statement to the effect that he had not taken insurance, and now realized his mistake. The statements were signed, "Thomas B. Lumpkin, General Agent." The picture of the plaintiff was taken from a negative obtained by the defendant Lumpkin, or some one by him authorized, from the defendant Adams, which was used with his consent and with knowledge of the purpose for which it was to be used. The picture was made from the negative without the plaintiff's consent, at the instance of the defendant insurance company, through its agent Lumpkin. Plaintiff is an artist by profession, and the publication is peculiarly offensive to him. The statement attributed to plaintiff in the publication is false and malicious. He never made any such statement, and has not and never has had a policy of life-insurance with the defendant company. The publication is malicious and tends to bring plaintiff into ridicule before the world, and especially with his friends and acquaintances who know that he has no policy in the defendant company. The publication is "a trespass upon plaintiff's right of privacy, and was caused by breach of confidence and trust reposed" in the defendant Adams.

JUSTICE COBB:

The petition really contains two counts; one for a libel, and the other for a violation of the plaintiff's right of privacy. . . . We will first deal with the general demurrer to the second count, which claimed damages on account of an alleged violation of the plaintiff's right of privacy. . . . It is to be conceded that prior to 1890 every adjudicated case, both in this country and in England, which might be said to have involved a right of privacy, was not based upon the existence of such right, but was founded upon a supposed right of property, or a breach of trust or confidence, or the like; and that therefore a claim to a right of privacy, independent of a property or contractual right or some right of a similar nature, had, up to that time, never been recognized in terms in any decision. The entire absence for a long period of time, even for centuries, of a precedent for an asserted right should have the effect to cause the courts to proceed with caution before recognizing the right, for fear that they may thereby invade the province of the lawmaking power; but such absence, even for all time, is not conclusive. . . . In such a case "although there be no precedent, the common law will judge according to the law of nature and the public good." Where the case is new in principle, the courts have no authority to give a remedy, no matter how great the grievance; but where the case is only new in instance, and the sole question is upon the application of a recognized principle to a new case, "it will be just as competent to courts of justice to apply the principle to any case that may arise two centuries hence as it was two centuries ago." Broom's Legal Maxims (8th ed.), 193. . . The individual surrenders to society many rights and privileges which he would be free to exercise in a state of nature, in exchange for the benefits which he receives as a member of society. But he is not presumed to surrender all those rights, and the public has no more right, without his consent, to invade the domain of those rights which it is necessarily to be presumed he has reserved than he has to violate the valid regulations of the organized government under which he lives. The right of privacy has its foundation in the instincts of nature. It is recognized intuitively, consciousness being the witness that can be called to establish its existence. Any person whose intellect is in a normal condition recognizes at once that as to each individual member of society there are matters private and there are matters public so far as the individual is concerned. Each individual as instinctively resents any encroachment by the public upon his rights which are of a private nature as he does the withdrawal of those of his rights which are of a public nature. A right of privacy in matters purely private is therefore derived from natural law. . . .

. . . Liberty includes the right to live as one will, so long as that will does not interfere with the rights of another or of the public. One may desire to live a life of seclusion; another may desire to live a life of publicity; still another may wish to live a life of privacy as to certain matters and of publicity as to others. . . .

All will admit that the individual who desires to live a life of seclusion cannot be compelled, against his consent, to exhibit his person in any public place, unless such exhibition is demanded by the law of the land. He may be required to come from his place of seclusion to perform public duties,—to serve as a juror and to testify as a witness, and the like; but when the public duty is once performed, if he excercises his liberty to go again into seclusion, no one can deny him the right. One who desires to live a life of partial seclusion has a right to choose the times, places, and manner in which and at which he will submit himself to the public gaze. Subject to the limitation above referred to, the body of a person cannot be put on exhibition at any time or at any place without his consent. . . . The right of privacy within certain limits is a right derived from natural law, recognized by the principles of municipal law, and guaranteed to persons in this State by the constitutions of the United States and of the State of Georgia, in those provisions which declare that no person shall be deprived of liberty except by due process of law.

. . . Ancient law recognized that a person had a legal right "to be let alone," so long as he was not interfering with the rights of other individuals or of the public. This idea has been carried into the common law, and appears from time to time in various places, a conspicuous instance being in the case of private nuisances resulting from noise which interferes with one's enjoyment of his home. . . .

The right of privacy, however, like every other right that rests in the individual, may be waived by him, or by any one authorized by him, or by any one whom the law empowers to act in his behalf, provided the effect of his waiver will not be such as to bring before the public those matters of a purely private nature which express law or public policy demands shall be kept private. . . . The most striking illustration of a waiver is where one either seeks or allows himself to be presented as a candidate for public office. He thereby waives any right to restrain or impede the public in any proper investigation into the conduct of his private life which may throw light upon his qualifications for the office or the advisability of imposing upon him the public trust which the office carries. But even in this case the waiver does not extend into those matters and transactions of private life which are wholly foreign and can throw no light whatever upon the question as to his competency for the office or the propriety of bestowing it upon him. . . .

It may be said that to establish a liberty of privacy would involve in numerous cases the perplexing question to determine where this liberty ended and the rights of others and of the public began. This affords no reason for not recognizing the liberty of privacy and giving to the person aggrieved legal redress against the wrong-doer in a case where it is clearly shown that a legal wrong has been done. It may be that there will arise many cases which lie near the border line which marks the right of privacy on the one hand and the right of another individual or of the public on the other. But this is true in regard to numerous other rights which the law recognizes as resting in the individual. In regard to cases that may arise under the right of privacy, as in cases that arise under other rights where the line of demarcation is to be determined, the safe-guard of the individual on the one hand and of the public on the other is the wisdom and integrity of the judiciary. . . .

The stumbling block which many have encountered in the way of a recognition of the existence of a right of privacy has been that the recognition of such right would inevitably tend to curtail the liberty of speech and of the press. This right to speak and the right of privacy have been coexistent. Each is a natural right, each exists, and each must be recognized and enforced with due respect for the other. . . .

Roberson v. Rochester Folding Box Company . . . before the Court of Appeals of New York in 1902, . . . is the first and only decision by a court of last resort involving directly the existence of a right of privacy. The decision was by a divided court. . . . While the ruling of the majority is limited in its effect to the unwarranted publication of the picture of another for advertising purposes, the reasoning of Judge Parker goes to the extent of denying the existence in the law of a right of privacy, "founded upon the claim that a man has a right to pass through this world without having his picture published, his business enterprises discussed, or his eccentricities commented upon, whether the comment be favorable or otherwise." The reasoning of the majority is, in substance, that there is no decided case either in England or in this country in which such a right is distinctly recognized; that every case that might be relied on to establish the right was placed expressly upon other grounds, not involving the application of this right in any sense; that the right is not referred to by the commentators and writers upon the common law or the principles of equity; that the existence of the right is not to be legitimately inferred from anything that is said by any of such writers; and that a recognition of the existence of the right would bring about a vast amount of litigation; and that in many instances where the right would be asserted it would be difficult, if not impossible, to determine the line of demarcation between the plaintiff's right of privacy and the well-established rights of others and of the public. . . . But we are utterly at variance with him in his conclusion that the existence of this right can not be legitimately inferred from what has been said by commentators upon the legal rights of individuals, and from expressions which have fallen from judges in their reasoning in cases where the exercise of the right was not directly involved. So far as the judgment in the case is based upon the argument *ab inconvenienti*,[20] all that is necessary to be said is that this argument has no place in the case if the right invoked has an existence in the law. . . . The true lawyer, when called to the discharge of judicial functions, has in all times, as a general rule, displayed remarkable conservatism; and wherever it was legally possible to base a judgment upon principles which had been recognized by a long course of judicial decision, this has been done, in preference to applying a principle which might be considered novel. It was for this reason that the numerous cases, both in England and in this country, which really protected the right of privacy were not placed upon the existence of this right, but were allowed to rest upon principles derived from the law of property, trust, and contract. Any candid mind will, however, be compelled to concede that in order to give relief in many of those cases it required a severe strain to bring them within the recognized rules which were sought to be applied. . . .

. . . The conclusion reached by us seems to be so thoroughly in accord with natural justice, with the principles of the law of every civilized nation, and especially with the elastic principles of the common law, and so thoroughly in harmony with those principles as molded under the influence of American institutions, that it seems strange to us that not only four of the judges of one of the most distinguished and learned courts of the Union, but also lawyers of learning and ability, have found an insurmountable stumbling-block in the path that leads to a recognition of the right which would give to persons like the plaintiff in this case, and the young woman in the Roberson case, redress for the legal wrong, or, what is by some of the lawwriters called, the outrage, perpetrated by the unauthorized use of their pictures for advertising purposes.

. . . There is in the publication of one's picture for advertising purposes not the slightest semblance of an expression of an idea, a thought, or an opinion,

---

[20] An argument from the inconvenience of the consequence.

within the meaning of the constitutional provision which guarantees to a person the right to publish his sentiments on any subject. Such conduct is not embraced within the liberty to print, but is a serious invasion of one's right of privacy. . . .

Justice Cobb's opinion in *Pavesich*, which has been called "one of the most dynamic and creative decisions in American jurisprudence," falls into three parts. First, a positive argument is offered in favor of the existence of the right of privacy. Second, the limits of the right of privacy and its relation to such rights as free speech and freedom of the press are treated. And third, the holding of *Roberson* is discussed and rejected. In its general, overall form, the structure of Cobb's main argument is quite simple:

> (i)   If there is a legal right of privacy, then individuals have a legal right not to have their pictures used for advertising purposes.
>
> (ii)  If individuals have a legal right not to have their pictures used for advertising purposes, then there is a cause of action on the facts alleged in the complaint.
>
> (iii) There is a legal right of privacy.
>
> (iv)  Therefore, there is a cause of action on the facts alleged in the complaint.

Strictly speaking, Cobb has to establish each of the three premises as true, acceptable, or correct.

In the light of our analysis of *Roberson*, it is clear that Chief Judge Parker would grant premise (i); but he denies its antecedent, that is, premise (iii). In barest outline Parker's argument runs:

> (i')   If there is a legal right of privacy, then individuals have a legal right not to be gossiped about (for example).
>
> (ii')  It is not the case that individuals have a legal right not to be gossiped about.
>
> (iii') Therefore, it is not the case that there is a legal right of privacy.

Because of this kind of argument, which encapsulates the issues of free speech and free press, Justice Cobb finds it necessary to consider the limits of the right of privacy; this topic is the second part of the opinion. The fact that it is difficult to draw a line between the individual's right of privacy and the rights of the public is no reason for refusing to grant relief to a party whose rights clearly have been violated, he maintains. Courts constantly face difficult line-drawing problems, and they deal with them fairly well. Moreover, there are limits to the rights of free speech and free press.

Plainly, however, it is the justification of premise (iii) that is crucial. (The second premise does not appear to be problematic.) Let us consider the main details of the first part of the opinion, with attention focused on the kinds of reasons Cobb gives for accepting (iii). (The third part of the opinion will not be discussed.) Cobb begins by delimiting the circumstances in which a court may introduce new rules into the law: it may not where the case is new in principle; it may when the case is a new application of a recognized principle of law. A subsidiary, direct argument is presented to show that there is, in principle, a right of privacy in the law.

The argument essentially is a piece of political and legal philosophy that is reminiscent of seventeenth- and eighteenth-century natural law doctrines. In entering society, the individual surrenders certain of his or her rights in exchange for benefits but retains certain other rights. Among these reserved natural rights is the right of privacy. This is intuitively recognized, and the distinction between the public and the private is preserved by a jealous instinct. Moreover, the retained right to life is the right to the enjoyment of life, which must include a right of privacy—the right to be left alone—as long as one respects the rights of others. To be sure, one may be compelled to perform public duties, and thereby be compelled to submit oneself to public gaze; but once these duties are performed, one may return to a life of seclusion. Put in other words, the individual, within limits, has control over his or her own life. This control is the sphere of personal liberty, the right of privacy. (Control over one's own life, of course, is tantamount to control over others; it entails the power to exclude others from intrusion into one's own life, as is the case, presumably, when one's picture is used for commercial purposes.) There is, then, a natural right of privacy.

But this right, Cobb maintains, is not merely a natural right: it is also a legal right. It is reflected in various principles of municipal law and constitutional provisions which declare that no person shall be deprived of liberty without due process of law. Due process of law, as Justice Cobb interprets it, is not only a procedural notion but also implicitly refers to substantive personal rights. The right of privacy, however, is not a right created by the civil law; it is an antecedent right that is protected by provisions of municipal and constitutional law. Rules of law regarding private nuisances and unreasonable searches and seizures cannot reasonably be said to be founded on a property right; such rules rather are implied recognition of a right of privacy. Therefore, although there may be no explicit mention of a right of privacy in the precedents, there is in principle a right of privacy in the law. Thus premise (iii) is justified.

It should be apparent that Cobb's reason for accepting (iii) is quite complex. It does not seem to be a straightforward goal-oriented reason, nor is it a straightforward rights-oriented reason—although the whole argument is concerned with rights. (The passage beginning with the legal right of privacy and ending with the right not to have one's picture used for advertising purposes is rights-oriented.) Perhaps we should think of Cobb's subsidiary argument as composed of two separate arguments, and therefore two separate reasons, one of which rests on an "appeal to natural law (or natural rights)" and the other of which rests on an "appeal to implicit legal rights."

The first of these might be viewed, arguably, as a special kind of goal-oriented practical argument that assumes a natural right of privacy:

(A) The natural right of privacy is a right that the law ought to protect.
(B) Legal recognition of a right to privacy is a necessary means to protection of the natural right.
(C) Therefore, the law ought to recognize a right to privacy.

Undoubtedly, Cobb does have something like this practical argument in mind, and his foray into political philosophy can be seen as an attempt to establish its first premise. Still, it may be slightly misleading to interpret the first subsidiary argument as constituting a goal-oriented kind of reason. For in the usual means-end relationship, the means are conceptually separable from the end; but here the relationship is one that approaches a tight intimacy. Legal recognition of the right of privacy is not just a means to the protection of the natural right. It, so to speak, flows from the natural right because natural law is incorporated into the civil law. If one wishes to view Cobb's reason as goal-oriented, it is a goal-oriented reason of a very special sort.

The second subsidiary argument appears to be a rights-oriented argument of a special kind. In the rights-oriented argument we hypothetically considered in the discussion of *Roberson*, the appeal goes from a supposed general legal right to a more specific legal right that is claimed to fall under it. Here, the appeal goes in the opposite direction. Cobb argues that the existence of a right of privacy in the law is shown by the fact, or so he claims, that certain rules of law (and therefore certain legal rights) presuppose the existence of a right of privacy. Put in other words, Justice Cobb is arguing that the *justification* of the right not to be subjected to unreasonable searches, for instance, is the right of privacy; therefore, the law in principle recognizes the right of privacy. (The traditional justification of the right not to be subjected to unreasonable searches on property-right grounds is attributable to the conservatism of lawyers, Cobb says.) Still it is not entirely clear that there is a sharp distinction between this second subsidiary argument and the first. For Cobb believes that the legal right not to be subjected to unreasonable searches is no more a creation of the civil law than is the right to privacy or the right to life. All these rights are part of the natural law and necessarily are incorporated into the civil law, lest the civil law be defective in a significant respect.

We have seen how two courts, on substantially the same set of facts, have arrived at opposite results. It would seem that Parker's argument in *Roberson* and Cobb's argument in *Pavesich* (taking "argument" to cover the premises that lead to the main conclusion and the reasons for accepting the premises) are both reasonable arguments. The question naturally arises, Which is the better argument? The disagreement between Parker and Cobb seems to turn on two basic points: (1) whether or not a right of privacy is a recognized principle of the law, and (2) whether or not the difficulty in drawing a principled distinction between legitimate and illegitimate claims to a right of privacy should bar the courts from granting relief to plaintiffs in *Roberson* and *Pavesich* situations. Regarding the disagreement on the first point, which to some extent is a disagreement over what the settled law is, it might not be easy to say who is right, Parker or Cobb. To the degree that Cobb's argument rests on the doctrine of antecedent natural rights, one might be reluctant to accept it. On the other hand, if it is hard for one to conceive that the law has no rational foundation in ethics and in political and legal philosophy, one might also be disposed towards Cobb's general approach. It is clear, at any rate, that judges do use, and perhaps inevitably do use, arguments that rely on ethical and general philosophical considerations.

On the second point one might lean toward Justice Cobb. Although judges ought to be principled in their decision making, for otherwise the process will be irrational and unobjective, it is probably unjust to deny Roberson and Pavesich their rights—and even Parker appears to concede that Roberson should have a right to relief from the intrusion—because it is difficult to draw a clear principled distinction between legitimate and illegitimate claims to privacy. Cobb, in fact, makes a valiant effort to stake out the boundaries; but the lines are not finely drawn. Perhaps it is impossible to do a better job in this problem area. In any event, neither opinion, Parker's nor Cobb's, is unreasonable.

But this statement leads to a paradox. If Parker and Cobb were both justified in reaching their respective decisions, and if they in a sense had a duty to render their particular decisions, then the law seems to allow that two incompatible statements of law can each be justified. What then is meant when one says that a proposition of law is true or correct? It would seem to be a condition for the meaningful application of the predicates "true" or "correct" to any given statement that these predicates should not also be applicable to the denial of the statement. This problem is part of the topic of "coherence," which cannot be taken up here.

It will be useful to summarize briefly the highlights of the part of this chapter that dealt with the kinds of reasons judges use to support a conclusion. (1) The kind of reason a judge has for the main conclusion of an opinion refers to why a judge thinks he is justified in accepting a premise of the main argument as true or correct. (2) Principally two kinds of reasons were discussed: goal-oriented and rights-oriented. (3) Various types of practical argument were distinguished. (4) The idea of principled decision was explained. (5) Judicial reasoning was shown to rest, at least in some cases, on value judgments or ethical and philosophical considerations.

It is important to emphasize that just as there are many more logical forms of argument than those we have noted, so also there may be many more kinds of reasons used by judges than the two on which we have focused. There are no official names for them. The reader, therefore, is invited to examine the opinions in the materials for this chapter and to identify, using any terminology he or she wishes, the kinds of reasons therein employed.

## MATERIALS

### Introduction

These materials contain excerpts from one article and a number of cases. The excerpt from the article by Warren and Brandeis, "The Right to Privacy," should be compared with the argument given by Justice Cobb in *Pavesich.*

Each of the cases should be analyzed in accordance with the method employed in this chapter's text. The following order is suggested: (1) Identify the question of law with which the opinion is concerned. (2) Identify the main conclusion of the opinion (i.e., the result of the case with respect to the question of law). (3) Identify the premises that are presented in support of the conclusion. Where necessary, state the assumptions that are being made by the judge. (4) Identify the logical form of the argument, using letters to stand for the terms (nouns or noun phrases) or the statements. Estimate the validity or strength of the argument (i.e., determine whether or not the premises entail the conclusion, or whether or not the premises, if true or correct, make the conclusion plausible. (5) Repeat the above steps for any other arguments contained in the opinion. (6) Identify the reasons given by the judge for accepting (or rejecting) any of the premises, and state whatever practical legal arguments are being used. (7) Identify the kinds of reasons. (8) Give your estimation as to whether the reasons are good reasons.

As stated in this chapter's text, there are no official names for the kinds of reasons used by judges, and readers will have to invent names of their own. The text concentrated primarily on goal-oriented and rights-oriented reasons, but there are other kinds. For instance, in *Sinkler v. Kneale* the court holds that an (alleged) change in medical knowledge necessitates changing a particular legal rule. And in *Summers v. Tice* the court argues in favor of a particular result, partly on grounds of "fairness." The "appeal to justice or fairness" is classified by Robert S. Summers, in the article referred to in the text, as a "rightness reason." These examples may suggest to the reader various ways of classifying reasons by kind.

It cannot be emphasized too strongly that the cases included in these materials are not aimed to teach the reader what the current law is on any issue. In some instances, the excerpts address only one question of law in a case, and no conclusion should be drawn about the final disposition of the question. The focus throughout should be on the process of judicial argumentation. As an aid to class discussion, each case is followed by a question or set of questions.

## Samuel D. Warren and Louis D. Brandeis, "The Right to Privacy" (1890)*

*"The Right to Privacy" by Samuel Warren and Louis Brandeis has been called "perhaps the most influential law review article of all."[†] It marked the first effort to establish a right of privacy founded in tort law. At the time the article was written, the authors were already recognized as outstanding lawyers and scholars. Both of them, as William L. Prosser notes, were "gifted with scholarship, imagination and ability." Yet, their motivation in writing the article was as much personal as it was scholarly.*

*In 1890, Warren and his wife lived in Boston, a very "proper" city, where people kept their personal lives to themselves. The Warrens were wealthy. Mr. Warren had*

---

* Samuel D. Warren and Louis D. Brandeis, "The Right to Privacy," *Harvard Law Review*, 4 (1890), p. 193.
† William L. Prosser, "Privacy," *California Law Review*, 48 (1960), p. 383.

*recently given up his law practice to devote full time to a paper manufacturing business he had inherited. Mrs. Warren was a prominent socialite who frequently gave large parties. To the great annoyance of the Warrens, these parties were covered in the Boston newspapers in embarrassing detail. Their annoyance came to a head when the newspapers had a field day on the occasion of the marriage of one of their daughters. Warren believed that he should have some legal protection against intrusions into his (and his wife's) personal life. He therefore got in touch with his former law partner, Brandeis (who was appointed to the U.S. Supreme Court in 1916), and together they wrote the article of which the following is an excerpt.*

That the individual shall have full protection in person and in property is a principle as old as the common law; but it has been found necessary from time to time to define anew the exact nature and extent of such protection. Political, social, and economic changes entail the recognition of new rights, and the common law, in its eternal youth, grows to meet the demands of society. . . .

Thus, with the recognition of the legal value of sensations, the protection against actual bodily injury was extended to prohibit mere attempts to do such injury; that is, the putting another in fear of such injury. From the action of battery grew that of assault. Much later there came a qualified protection of the individual against offensive noises and odors, against dust and smoke, and excessive vibration. The law of nuisance was developed. So regard for human emotions soon extended the scope of personal immunity beyond the body of the individual. His reputation, the standing among his fellowmen, was considered, and the law of slander and libel arose. Man's family relations became a part of the legal conception of his life, and the alienation of a wife's affections was held remediable. Occasionally the law halted,—as in its refusal to recognize the intrusion by seduction upon the honor of the family. But even here the demands of society were met. A mean fiction, the action per quod servitium amisit,* was resorted to, and by allowing damages for injury to the parents' feelings, an adequate remedy was ordinarily afforded. Similar to the expansion of the right to life was the growth of the legal conception of property. From corporeal property arose the incorporeal rights issuing out of it; and then there opened the wide realm of intangible property, in the products and processes of the mind, as works of literature and art, goodwill, trade secrets, and trademarks.

---

\* An *action per quod servitium amisit* literally means an action "whereby the servant was lost." It was used under old rules of pleading in actions for trespass brought by a master. It described the special damages the master suffered because of the defendant's alleged beating or misuse of the master's servant.

This development of the law was inevitable. The intense intellectual and emotional life, and the heightening of sensations which came with the advance of civilization, made it clear to men that only a part of the pain, pleasure, and profit of life lay in physical things. Thoughts, emotions, and sensations demanded legal recognition, and the beautiful capacity for growth which characterizes the common law enabled the judges to afford the requisite protection, without the interposition of the legislature.

Recent inventions and business methods call attention to the next step which must be taken for the protection of the person, and for securing to the individual what Judge Cooley calls the right "to be let alone." Instantaneous photographs and newspaper enterprise have invaded the sacred precincts of private and domestic life; and numerous mechanical devices threaten to make good the prediction that "what is whispered in the closet shall be proclaimed from the house-tops." . . .

Of the desirability—indeed of the necessity—of some such protection, there can, it is believed, be no doubt. The press is overstepping in every direction the obvious bounds of propriety and of decency. Gossip is no longer the resource of the idle and of the vicious, but has become a trade, which is pursued with industry as well as effrontery. To satisfy a prurient taste, the details of sexual relations are spread broadcast in the columns of the daily papers. To occupy the indolent, column upon column is filled with idle gossip, which can only be procured by intrusion upon the domestic circle. The intensity and complexity of life, attendant upon advancing civilization, have rendered necessary some retreat from the world, and man, under the refining influence of culture, has become more sensitive to publicity, so that solitude and privacy have become more essential to the individual; but modern enterprise and invention have, through invasions upon his privacy, subjected him to mental pain and distress, far greater than could be inflicted by mere bodily injury. . . .

It is our purpose to consider whether the existing law affords a principle which can properly be invoked to protect the privacy of the individual; and, if it does, what the nature and extent of such protection is.

Owing to the nature of the instruments by which privacy is invaded, the injury inflicted bears a superficial resemblance to the wrongs dealt with by the law of slander and of libel, while a legal remedy for such injury seems to involve the treatment of mere wounded feelings, as a substantive cause of action. The principle on which the law of defamation rests, covers, however, a radically different class of effects from those for which attention is now asked. It deals only with damage to reputation, with the injury done to the individual in his external relations to the community, by lowering him

in the estimation of his fellows. The matter published of him, however wide-
ly circulated, and however unsuited to publicity, must, in order to be ac-
tionable, have a direct tendency to injure him in his intercourse with others,
and even if in writing or in print, must subject him to the hatred, ridicule, or
contempt of his fellowmen,—the effect of the publication upon his estimate
of himself and upon his own feelings not forming an essential element in the
cause of action. . . . On the other hand, our law recognizes no principle upon
which compensation can be granted for mere injury to the feelings. . . . Injury of feelings may indeed be taken account of in ascertaining the amount of
damages when attending what is recognized as a legal injury; but our
system, unlike the Roman law, does not afford a remedy even for mental
suffering which results from mere contumely and insult, from an intentional
and unwarranted violation of the "honor" of another.

   It is not however necessary, in order to sustain the view that the common
law recognizes and upholds a principle applicable to cases of invasion of privacy, to invoke the analogy, which is but superficial, to injuries sustained,
either by an attack upon reputation or by what the civilians called a violation
of honor; for the legal doctrines relating to infractions of what is ordinarily
termed the common-law right to intellectual and artistic property are, it is
believed, but instances and applications of a general right to privacy, which
properly understood afford a remedy for the evils under consideration.

   The common law secured to each individual the right of determining, ordinarily, to what extent his thoughts, sentiments, and emotions shall be com-
municated to others. . . . The same protection is accorded to a casual letter
or an entry in a diary and to the most valuable poem or essay, to a botch or
daub and to a masterpiece. In every such case the individual is entitled to
decide whether that which is his shall be given to the public. No other has
the right to publish his productions in any form, without his consent. . . .
The right is lost only when the author himself communicates his production
to the public,—in other words, publishes it. It is entirely independent of the
copyright laws, and their extension into the domain of art. . . . The statutory
right is of no value, *unless* there is a publication; the common-law right is
lost *as soon as* there is a publication.

   What is the nature, the basis, of this right to prevent the publication of
manuscripts or works of art? It is stated to be the enforcement of a right of
property, and no difficulty arises in accepting this view, so long as we have
only to deal with the reproduction of literary and artistic compositions. . . .
But where the value of the production is found not in the right to take the
profits arising from publication, but in the peace of mind or the relief afforded by the ability to prevent any publication at all, it is difficult to regard the
right as one of property, in the common acceptation of that term. . . .

That this protection cannot rest upon the right to literary or artistic property in any exact sense, appears the more clearly when the subject-matter for which protection is invoked is not even in the form of intellectual property, but has the attributes of ordinary tangible property. Suppose a man has a collection of gems or curiosities which he keeps private; it would hardly be contended that any person could publish a catalogue of them, and yet the articles enumerated are certainly not intellectual property in the legal sense, any more than a collection of stoves or of chairs.

. . . It may now be considered settled that the protection afforded by the common law to the author of any writing is entirely independent of its pecuniary value, its intrinsic merits, or of any intention to publish the same, and, of course, also, wholly independent of the material, if any, upon which, or the mode in which, the thought or sentiment was expressed.

Although the courts have asserted that they rested their decisions on the narrow grounds of protection to property, yet there are recognitions of a more liberal doctrine. . . . Lord Cottenham stated that a man "is entitled to be protected in the exclusive use and enjoyment of that which is exclusively his," and cited with approval the opinion of Lord Eldon, as reported in a manuscript note of the case of Wyatt v. Wilson, in 1820, respecting an engraving of George the Third during his illness, to the effect that "if one of the late king's physicians had kept a diary of what he heard and saw, the court would not, in the king's lifetime, have permitted him to print and publish it;" and Lord Cottenham declared, in respect to the acts of the defendants in the case before him, that "privacy is the right invaded." But if privacy is once recognized as a right entitled to legal protection, the interposition of the courts cannot depend on the particular nature of the injuries resulting.

These considerations lead to the conclusion that the protection afforded to thoughts, sentiments, and emotions, expressed through the medium of writing or of the arts, so far as it consists in preventing publication, is merely an instance of the enforcement of the more general right of the individual to be let alone. . . . The principle which protects personal writings and all other personal productions, not against theft and physical appropriation, but against publication in any form, is in reality not the principle of private property, but that of an inviolate personality.

If we are correct in this conclusion, the existing law affords a principle which may be invoked to protect the privacy of the individual from invasion. . . . If, then, the decisions indicate a general right to privacy for thoughts, emotions, and sensations, these should receive the same protection, whether expressed in writing, or in conduct, in conversation, in attitudes, or in facial expression.

It may be urged that a distinction should be taken between the deliberate expression of thoughts and emotions in literary or artistic compositions and the casual and often involuntary expression given to them in the ordinary conduct of life. In other words, it may be contended that the protection afforded is granted to the conscious products of labor, perhaps as an encouragement to effort. This contention, however plausible, has, in fact, little to recommend it. If the amount of labor involved be adopted as the test, we might well find that the effort to conduct one's self properly in business and in domestic relations had been far greater than that involved in painting a picture or writing a book; one would find that it was far easier to express lofty sentiments in a diary than in the conduct of a noble life. If the test of deliberateness of the act be adopted, much casual correspondence which is now accorded full protection would be excluded from the beneficent operation of existing rules. After the decisions denying the distinction attempted to be made between those literary productions which it was intended to publish and those which it was not, all considerations of the amount of labor involved, the degree of deliberation, the value of the product, and the intention of publishing must be abandoned, and no basis is discerned upon which the right to restrain publication and reproduction of such so-called literary and artistic works can be rested, except the right to privacy, as a part of the more general right to the immunity of the person,—the right to one's personality.

It should be stated that, in some instances where protection has been afforded against wrongful publication, the jurisdiction has been asserted, not on the ground of property, or at least not wholly on that ground, but on the ground of an alleged breach of an implied contract or of a trust or confidence.

Thus, in Abernethy v. Hutchinson, 3 L.J.Ch. 209 (1825), where the plaintiff, a distinguished surgeon, sought to restrain the publication in the "Lancet" of unpublished lectures which he had delivered at St. Bartholomew's Hospital in London, Lord Eldon doubted whether there could be property in lectures which had not been reduced to writing, but granted the injunction on the ground of breach of confidence, holding "that when persons were admitted as pupils or otherwise, to hear these lectures, although they were orally delivered, and although the parties might go to the extent, if they were able to do so, of putting down the whole by means of short-hand, yet they could do that only for the purposes of their own information, and could not publish, for profit, that which they had not obtained the right of selling." . . .

This process of implying a term in a contract, or of implying a trust (particularly where the contract is written, and where there is no established usage or custom), is nothing more nor less than a judicial declaration that public morality, private justice, and general convenience demand the recognition of such a rule, and that the publication under similar circumstances would be considered an intolerable abuse. So long as these circumstances happen to present a contract upon which such a term can be engrafted by the judicial mind, or to supply relations upon which a trust or confidence can be erected, there may be no objection to working out the desired protection through the doctrines of contract or of trust. But the court can hardly stop there. The narrower doctrine may have satisfied the demands of society at a time when the abuse to be guarded against could rarely have arisen without violating a contract or a special confidence; but now that modern devices afford abundant opportunities for the perpetration of such wrongs without any participation by the injured party, the protection granted by the law must be placed upon a broader foundation. . . . The right of property in its widest sense, including all possession, including all rights and privileges, and hence embracing the right to an inviolate personality, affords alone that broad basis upon which the protection which the individual demands can be rested.

Thus, the courts, in searching for some principle upon which the publication of private letters could be enjoined, naturally came upon the ideas of a breach of confidence, and of an implied contract; but it required little consideration to discern that this doctrine could not afford all the protection required, since it would not support the court in granting a remedy against a stranger; and so the theory of property in the contents of letters was adopted. . . .

A similar groping for the principle upon which a wrongful publication can be enjoined is found in the law of trade secrets. There, injunctions have generally been granted on the theory of a breach of contract, or of an abuse of confidence. It would, of course, rarely happen that any one would be in the possession of a secret unless confidence had been reposed in him. But can it be supposed that the court would hesitate to grant relief against one who had obtained his knowledge by an ordinary trespass,—for instance, by wrongfully looking into a book in which the secret was recorded, or by eavesdropping? . . .

We must therefore conclude that the rights, so protected, whatever their exact nature, are not rights arising from contract or from special trust, but are rights as against the world; and, as above stated, the principle which has been applied to protect these rights is in reality not the principle of private property, unless that word be used in an extended and unusual sense. The principle which protects personal writings and any other productions of the intellect or of the emotions, is the right to privacy, and the law has no new principle to formulate when it extends this protection to the personal appearance, sayings, acts, and to personal relation, domestic or otherwise.

If the invasion of privacy constitutes a legal injuria, the elements for demanding redress exist, since already the value of mental suffering, caused by an act wrongful in itself, is recognized as a basis for compensation. . . .

It remains to consider what are the limitations of this right to privacy, and what remedies may be granted for the enforcement of the right. To determine in advance of experience the exact line at which the dignity and convenience of the individual must yield to the demands of the public welfare or of private justice would be a difficult task; but the more general rules are furnished by the legal analogies already developed in the law of slander and libel, and in the law of literary and artistic property. . . .

. . . The common law has always recognized a man's house as his castle, impregnable, often, even to its own officers engaged in the execution of its commands. Shall the courts thus close the front entrance to constituted authority, and open wide the back door to idle or prurient curiosity?

## QUESTIONS

1.   The authors base the right of privacy on (or perhaps identify this right with) the idea of "inviolate personality." What does this phrase mean?

2.   The article is "concerned only with public disclosure in the press of truthful but private details about the individual which caused emotional upset to him."[*] The *Pavesich* case, which favorably cites this article, is concerned with the commercial use of someone's picture without his consent. Should both of these issues be thought of as falling under one broad "right of privacy," or are they quite distinct issues?

## *Roberson v. Rochester Folding Box* ═══════════════
## *Co. (1902),*
## *Dissenting Opinion*[†]

*Roberson was decided by a vote of 4 to 3. The following is an excerpt from the dissenting opinion.*

---

* Harry S. Kalven, "Privacy in Tort Law—Were Warren and Brandeis Wrong?" *Law and Contemporary Problems*, 31 (1966), pp. 330.

† 171 N.Y. 538 (1902).

JUDGE GRAY:

Instantaneous photography is a modern invention. . . . If it is to be permitted that the portraiture may be put to commercial, or other, uses for gain, by the publication of prints therefrom, then an act of invasion of the individual's privacy results, possibly more formidable and more painful in its consequences, than an actual bodily assault might be. Security of person is as necessary as security of property; and for the complete personal security, which will result in the peaceful and wholesome enjoyment of one's privileges as a member of society, there should be afforded protection, not only against the scandalous portraiture and display of one's features and person, but against the display and use thereof for another's commercial purposes or gain. The proposition is, to me, an inconceivable one that these defendants may, unauthorizedly, use the likeness of this young woman upon their advertisement, as a method of attracting widespread public attention to their wares, and that she must submit to the mortifying notoriety, without right to invoke the exercise of the preventive power of a court of equity.

Such a view, as it seems to me, must have been unduly influenced by a failure to find precedents in analogous cases, or some declaration by the great commentators upon the law of a common-law principle which would, precisely, apply to and govern the action; without taking into consideration that, in the existing state of society, new conditions affecting the relations of persons demand the broader extension of those legal principles, which underlie the immunity of one's person from attack. I think that such a view is unduly restricted, too, by a search for some property, which has been invaded by the defendants' acts. Property is not necessarily the thing itself, which is owned; it is the right of the owner in relation to it. . . . I think that this plaintiff has the same property in the right to be protected against the use of her face for defendants' commercial purposes, as she would have, if they were publishing her literary compositions. The right would be conceded if she sat for her photograph; but if her face or her portraiture, has a value, the value is hers exclusively; until the use be granted away to the public. Any other principle of decision, in my opinion, is as repugnant to equity as it is shocking to reason. . . .

## QUESTION

1. In the majority opinion Judge Parker wrote: "The legislative body could very well interfere and arbitrarily provide that no one should be permitted for his own selfish purpose to use the picture or the name of another for advertising purposes without his consent. In such event, no embarrassment would result to the general body of the law, for the rule would be applicable only to cases provided for by the statute. The

courts, however, being without authority to legislate, are required to decide cases upon principle, and so are necessarily embarrassed by precedents created by an extreme, and therefore, unjustifiable application of an old principle." Compare this remark with Judge Gray's dissent. Has Judge Gray formulated a principle that will not "embarrass" courts in future cases? If so, what is the principle?

## Riggs v. Palmer (1889)*

*The case of* Riggs v. Palmer *raises the issue of whether a court is justified in deciding a case by employing a principle of justice or morality, even if doing so means the decision is contrary to the letter of the written law. In* Riggs v. Palmer, *one of the defendants (Elmer Palmer, aged sixteen) murdered his grandfather so that he would not be cut out of his grandfather's will. When Elmer Palmer claimed his inheritance, two other relatives challenged his right to inherit. Here is an excerpt from the majority opinion of the New York Court of Appeals in the case.*

JUDGE EARL:

[Elmer Palmer says that the] will was made made in due form, and has been admitted to probate; and that therefore it must have effect according to the letter of the law. It is quite true that statutes regulating the making, proof, and effect of wills and the devolution of property, if literally construed, and if their force and effect can in no way and under no circumstances be controlled or modified, give this property to the murderer. The purpose of those statutes was to enable testators† to dispose of their estates to the objects of their bounty at death, and to carry into effect their final wishes legally expressed; and in considering and giving effect to them this purpose must be kept in view. It was the intention of the lawmakers that the *donees*‡ in a will should have the property given to them. But it never could have been their intention that a *donee* who murdered the testator to make the will operative should have any benefit under it. If such a case had been present to their minds, and it had been supposed necessary to make some provision of law to meet it, it cannot be doubted that they would have provided for it. It is a familiar canon of construction that a thing which is within the intention of the makers of a statute is as much within the statute as if it were within the letter; and a thing which is within the letter of the statute is not within the statute unless it be within the intention of the makers. . . .

What could be more unreasonable than to suppose that it was the

---

* 115 N.Y. 506, 22 N.E. 188 (1889).

† A *testator* is a person who has died and left a will.

‡ In this context, *donee* means one to whom a gift is made or a bequest is given.

legislative intention in the general laws passed for the orderly, peaceable, and just devolution of property that they should have operation in favor of one who murdered his ancestor that he might speedily come into the possession of his estate? Such an intention is inconceivable. We need not, therefore, be much troubled by the general language contained in the laws. Besides, all laws, as well as all contracts, may be controlled in their operation and effect by general, fundamental maxims of the common law. No one shall be permitted to profit by his own fraud, or to take advantage of his own wrong, or to found any claim upon his own iniquity, or to acquire property by his own crime. These maxims are dictated by public policy, have their foundation in universal law administered in all civilized countries, and have nowhere been superseded by statutes. They were applied in the decision of the case of Insurance Co. v. Armstrong, 117 U.S. 599, 6 S.Ct. 877. There it was held that the person who procured a policy upon the life of another, payable at his death, and then murdered the assured to make the policy payable, could not recover thereon. Mr. Justice Field writing the opinion, said: "Independently of any proof of the motives of Hunter in obtaining the policy, and even assuming that they were just and proper, he forfeited all rights under it when, to secure its immediate payment, he murdered the assured. It would be a reproach to the jurisprudence of the country if one could recover insurance money payable on the death of a party whose life he had feloniously taken. As well might he recover insurance money upon a building that he had willfully fired." These maxims, without any statute giving them force or operation, frequently control the effect and nullify the language of wills. . . .

. . . The will spoke and became operative at the death of the testator. [Elmer Palmer] caused that death, and thus by his crime made it speak and have operation. Shall it speak and operate in his favor? If he had met the testator, and taken his property by force, he would have had no title to it. Shall he acquire title by murdering him? If he had gone to the testator's house, and by force compelled him, or by fraud of undue influence had induced him, to will him his property, the law would not allow him to hold it. But can he give effect and operation to a will by murder, and yet take the property? To answer these questions in the affirmative it seems to me would be a reproach to the jurisprudence of our state, and an offense against public policy. . . .

. . . My view of this case does not inflict upon Elmer any greater or other punishment for his crime than the law specifies. It takes from him no property, but simply holds that he shall not acquire property by his crime, and thus be rewarded for its commission.

## QUESTIONS

1.  Judge Earl refers to "fundamental maxims of the common law" and says that these maxims may control all laws. If no statute gives these maxims their legal force, what is it that confers legal authority on them?
2.  Is it true that the law never permits people to profit from their own wrongdoing?
3.  In a dissenting opinion in this case, Judge Gray acknowledges that there are jurisdictions in which a heir is excluded by law from benefiting from a will if he has been convicted of killing, or attempting to kill, the testator. However, he goes on to write: "In the absence of such legislation here, the courts are not empowered to institute such a system of remedial justice. . . . The statutes of this state have prescribed various ways in which a will may be altered or revoked; but the very provision defining the modes of alteration and revocation implies a prohibition of alteration or revocation in any other way . . . the making and the revocation of a will are purely matters of statutory regulation. . . ." In practical effect, Gray says, the court was being asked to make another will for the testator, but "the laws do not warrant this judicial action." Since the majority opinion concedes that the meaning of the statutes governing wills is clear, do you think that Gray is right in maintaining that the court exceeded its powers in going beyond the literal meaning and ruling against the grandson, Elmer Palmer? Did the court usurp the powers of the legislature? Explain your answer.

## *Oleff v. Hodapp (1935)*[*]

*This case involves a Greek immigrant (Apostol) who opened a bank account in Dayton, Ohio. He made his nephew (Tego) a joint owner of the account. (Under a joint ownership arrangement, each individual has a legal right to the entire account. If one of the owners dies, the survivor possesses the whole account.) Apostol returned to Europe, where he was murdered. Tego was found guilty of being the "moral author of the crime" (although he did not do the actual killing). After Apostol's death, some of his heirs claimed the money he had deposited in his Ohio account. But Tego's representative in Ohio argued against their claim. He maintained that Tego was a joint owner of the account before Apostol's death (and therefore had a legal right to all the money before the murder) and so could not lose his ownership by being found guilty of the murder. Here are excerpts from the decision of the Supreme Court of Ohio.*

[*] 129 Ohio 432 (1935).

JUSTICE STEPHENSON:

. . . There is no statutory law in Ohio that deprives Tego of his right to this account. Counsel insist that Tego's right should be denied him because to allow it would be in contravention of sound public policy and place a premium on murder. We are not subscribing to the righteousness of Tego's legal status; but this is a court of law and not a theological institution. . . . Property cannot be taken from an individual who is legally entitled to it because he violated public policy. Property rights are too sacred to be subjected to a danger of that character. We experience no satisfaction in holding that Tego is entitled to this account; but that is the law and we must so find.

JUSTICE ZIMMERMAN, concurring:

It is with reluctance that I am constrained to concur in the majority opinion. If this were a case where Tego's right to the money was through inheritance, or by will, I should feel strongly urged to deny him that right on the ground, "that no one shall be permitted to take advantage of his own wrong. . . ." But Tego had a present joint interest in the deposit equal to Apostol's—a property right in the whole deposit prior to Apostol's death. . . .

How can we logically take his own property away from him?

## QUESTIONS

1. Is this case different from *Riggs v. Palmer*?
2. A dissenting judge in the case writes: "It is only by the court's aid that he can enjoy the profits of his wrongful deed." Do you agree that the court is allowing Tego to profit from his crime?

## *Depue v. Flateau (1907)**

*The plaintiff in* Depue v. Flateau *was a cattle buyer who went to the defendant's house to conduct business one cold day in Minnesota in January 1905. The Flateau house was about seven miles from his own house. He arrived about five o'clock in the evening, but it was too dark to inspect properly the cattle Flateau, Sr., had for sale. Depue asked if he could stay overnight in order to continue their business in the morning. Flateau refused this request. The plaintiff subsequently bought some furs from the Flateau family and accepted an invitation to eat dinner. After dinner Depue became ill. At this point the facts are in dispute, but it was "clear that he was seriously ill and too weak to take care of himself." Nevertheless, Flateau, Jr., assisted Depue to his sleigh and, upon seeing that Depue was too weak to hold the reins of his horses, placed the reins around Depue's shoulders. Flateau, Jr. then sent the horses in the*

* 100 Minn. 299, 111 N.W. 1 (1907).

*direction of Depue's house. Depue fell off the sleigh about three-quarters of a mile from the defendant's house. He was too weak to move and nearly froze to death. He was found the next morning and revived. His injuries required the amputation of several fingers.*

*Depue then sued the Flateaus, claiming they were negligent in sending him home on his own even though they knew his condition. The trial court dismissed the case on the grounds that Depue had not stated a cause of action (facts sufficient to state grounds for holding the defendant liable). The case came before the Supreme Court of Minnesota on appeal.*

JUSTICE BROWN:

. . . The case is an unusual one on its facts, and "all-four" precedents* are difficult to find in the books. In fact, after considerable research, we have found no case whose facts are identical with those at bar. It is insisted by defendants that they owed plaintiff no duty to entertain him during the night in question, and were not guilty of any negligent misconduct in refusing him accommodations, or in sending him home under the circumstances disclosed. Reliance is had for support of this contention upon the general rule as stated in Union Pacific Ry. Co. v. Cappier, 66 Kan. 649, 72 P. 281, 69 L.R.A. 513, where the court said: "Those duties which are dictated merely by good morals or by humane considerations are not within the domain of the law. Feelings of kindness and sympathy may move the Good Samaritan to minister to the sick and wounded at the roadside, but the law imposes no such obligation; and suffering humanity has no legal complaint against those who pass by on the other side. . . . Unless a relation exists between the sick, helpless, or injured and those who witness their distress, of a nature to require and impose upon them the duty of providing the necessary relief, there is neither legal obligation to minister on the one hand, nor cause for legal complaint on the other." This is no doubt a correct statement of the general rule applicable to the Good Samaritan, but it by no means controls a case like that at bar. The facts of this case bring it within the more comprehensive principle that whenever a person is placed in such a position with regard to another that it is obvious that, if he does not use due care in his own conduct, he will cause injury to that person, the duty at once arises to exercise care commensurate with the situation in which he thus finds himself, and with which he is confronted, to avoid such danger; and a negligent failure to perform the duty renders him liable for the consequences of his neglect. This principle applies to varied situations arising from non-contract relations. It protects the trespasser from wanton or willful injury. It

---

* *All-four precedents* are previous cases that are similar in all material respects to the case before the court.

extends to the licensee,* and requires the exercise of reasonable care to avoid an unnecessary injury to him. It imposes upon the owner of premises, which he expressly or impliedly invites persons to visit, whether for the transaction of business or otherwise, the obligation to keep the same in reasonably safe condition for use, though it does not embrace those sentimental or social duties often prompting human action. . . .

In the case at bar, defendants were under no contract obligation to minister to plaintiff in his distress; but humanity demanded that they do so, if they understood and appreciated his condition. And, though those acts which humanity demands are not always legal obligations, the rule to which we have adverted applied to the relation existing between these parties on this occasion and protected plaintiff from acts at their hands that would expose him to personal harm. He was not a trespasser upon their premises, but, on the contrary, was there by the express invitation of Flateau, Sr. He was taken suddenly ill while their guest, and the law, as well as humanity, required that he be not exposed in his helpless condition to the merciless elements. . . .

. . . If defendants knew and appreciated his condition, their act in sending him out to make his way to Medelia the best he could was wrongful and rendered them liable in damages. We do not wish to be understood as holding that defendants were under absolute duty to entertain plaintiff during the night. Whether they could conveniently do so does not appear. What they should or could have done in the premises can only be determined from a full view of the evidence disclosing their situation, and their facilities for communicating his condition to his friends, or near neighbors, if any there were. All these facts will enable the jury to determine whether, within the rules of negligence applicable to the case, defendants neglected any duty they owed plaintiff.

Order reversed.

## QUESTIONS

1. According to Justice Brown, what distinguishes the situation of the defendants from the situation of the Good Samaritan?
2. Should people have to act as Good Samaritans when the opportunity arises? Justify your answer.
3. Should the law require people, on pain of punishment or risk of liability (as in *Depue*) to act as Good Samaritans? Justify your answer.

---

* A *licensee* is a person who is legally entitled to be on another's land for his own purposes by virtue of the owner's express or implied consent.

## Summers v. Tice (1948)*

*Summers, Tice, and Simonson were part of the same hunting party. Tice and Simonson negligently fired their guns at the same time. They shot at quail in Summers's direction. Summers was struck in the eye by a shot from one gun, but it was impossible to determine which hunter fired the shot that caused the injury. Summers sued both Tice and Simonson, claiming that they should be considered as one unit so that Summers might recover damages even though he could not prove which hunter was responsible. The decision of the Supreme Court of California held that it was not necessary to use the artificial construction of viewing two hunters as one unit in order to hold both Tice and Simonson liable. Here is an excerpt from the court's opinion.*

JUSTICE CARTER:

. . . The problem presented in this case is whether the judgment against both defendants may stand. . . .

It has been held that where a group of persons are on a hunting party, or otherwise engaged in the use of firearms, and two of them are negligent in firing in the direction of a third person who is injured thereby, both of those so firing are liable for the injury suffered by the third person, although the negligence of only one of them could have caused the injury. [Citations omitted.] . . .

These cases speak of the action of defendants as being in concert as the ground of decision, yet it would seem they are straining that concept. . . .

When we consider the relative position of the parties and the results that would flow if plaintiff was required to pin the injury on one of the defendants only, a requirement that the burden of proof on that subject be shifted to defendants becomes manifest. They are both wrongdoers—both negligent toward plaintiff. They brought about a situation where the negligence of one of them injured the plaintiff, hence it should rest with them each to absolve himself if he can. The injured party has been placed by defendants in the unfair position of pointing to which defendant caused the harm. If one can escape the other may also and plaintiff is remediless. Ordinarily defendants are in a far better position to offer evidence to determine which one caused the injury. This reasoning has recently found favor in this Court. In a quite analogous situation this Court held that a patient injured while unconscious on an operating table in a hospital could hold all or any of the persons who had any connection with the operation even though he could not select the particular acts by the particular person which led to his disability. Ybarra v. Spangard, 25 Cal.2d 486, 154 P.2d 687.

. . . The wrongdoers should be left to work out between themselves any apportionment [of the damages].

The judgment is affirmed.

* 33 Cal.2d 80, 199 P.2d 1 (1948).

## QUESTIONS

1. The court thinks it would be unfair to the plaintiff to make him prove which defendant caused the injury. Is it unfair to the defendant who did not cause the injury (even if he cannot be identified) to make him contribute toward payment of the damages? If so, why?

2. Suppose the hunting party had had ten people, all of whom negligently fired their guns at the same time. Should they all be held liable, even though the likelihood that any one of them shot Summers is now smaller?

## *Sinkler v. Kneale (1960)**

*The court in* Sinkler v. Kneale *had to decide whether a child could sue for an injury allegedly suffered while a nonviable fetus. In this case, a mother who was one month pregnant was involved in an accident and allegedly injured when another car hit the car she was driving. The fetus she was carrying was subsequently born with Down's syndrome (commonly known as mongolism). The mother and others involved in the accident filed suit on their own behalf, claiming that the other driver was negligent. A suit was also filed on behalf of the Down's syndrome child. That suit alleged that she "was born Mongoloid as a result of injuries received in (the) automobile collision." At the trial, the defendant objected to this child's claim. The judge sustained the objection, ruling that since she was a nonviable fetus at the time of the accident, she could not have a right of action. The decision was appealed to the Supreme Court of Pennsylvania, which reinstated the claim. Here are excerpts from the majority opinion and a dissenting opinion. We begin with Justice Bok's consideration of a precedential case.*

JUSTICE BOK:

The parent case, both in this country and in England, is the Massachusetts decision first above cited, Dietrich v. Inhabitants of Northampton, where Judge Holmes in 1884 denied the right of action. He not only found no common law doctrine against it but felt it necessary to find some opposition to a statement by Lord Coke in the criminal law which is repeated by Blackstone at Book IV, p. 198.:

"To kill a child in its mother's womb is now no murder, but a great misprision:[†] but if the child be born alive and dieth by reason of the potion or bruises it received in the womb, it is murder in such as administered or gave them."

Even if the criminal law is faint authority for a tort, the foregoing must show at least that the common law offers no bar to the suit. Judge Holmes's

---

* 401 Pa.267, 164 A.2d 93 (1960)

† A *misprision* is an offense that does not have a specific name and is not specifically defined.

real point d'appui [point of support] for decision was that the unborn child was part of its mother. This was undoubtedly the medical view accepted by law at the time, and it is precisely the view that has altered since. . . .

The real catalyst of the problem is the current state of medical knowledge on the point of the separate existence of a foetus. In the Smith case Justice Proctor, speaking for the New Jersey Supreme Court in a unanimous decision, said this [31 N.J. 353, 157 A.2d 502]:

"The third reason for the rule denying recovery was the theory that an unborn child was a part of the mother, and therefore not a person in being to whom a duty of care could be owed. All the courts that have permitted recovery for prenatal injuries have disagreed with that theory. They found that the existence of an infant separate from its mother begins before birth, . . . Medical authorities have long recognized that a child is in existence from the moment of conception, and not merely a part of its mother's body." . . .

As for the notion that the child must have been viable when the injuries were received, which has claimed the attention of several of the states, we regard it as having little to do with the basic right to recover, when the foetus is regarded as having existence as a separate creature from the moment of conception. Even Judge Holmes said, in Dietrich, that "the argument would not be affected by the degree of maturity reached by the embryo at the moment of the organic lesion or wrongful act." The question is primarily one of causation, and since medical proof of that is necessary, we now remove the bars from it *in limine* [at the beginning of the trial].

The order is reversed.

JUSTICE BELL, dissenting:

. . . *The record does not show*, nor have we been informed of any development in modern medicine *in the last 20 years* which would justify any change in our decisional law. The majority opinion has gone outside the record to state that medical opinion has altered since the leading case of Dietrich v. Inhabitants of Northampton, 1884, 138 Mass. 14, and "the real catalyst of the problem is the current state of medical knowledge on the point of the separate existence of a foetus." In my judgment that is not the real and certainly it is not the sole important question. I regret that the majority did not conduct its off-the-record study further to determine (1) whether medical knowledge and science has changed on the point here involved in the last 20 years, and (2) whether trauma can cause an unborn child to become a Mongoloid. If such a study had been made, the majority would have discovered (1) that there has been no change on this point in medical knowledge and science in the last 20 years, and (2) that leading medical authorities are agreed (a) that a Mongoloid child is a Mongoloid from the time of its conception and results from the genes of the parents, and (b) that trauma cannot cause a child to become or be born a Mongoloid. . . . Negligence cases are swamping our Courts; families are drawing farther and farther apart—why create and greatly increase litigation and give new causes for family discord? Furthermore, in claims for shock, nervous disorders, allergies, malformations, feeble mindedness and many other real or imaginary injuries or illnesses, whether the alleged negligence of the defendant was the *proximate cause** of the prenatal injury, or illness or mental or physical defect, or what the physical, mental or nervous condition of the child was at the time of the accident and while en ventre sa mere [in its mother's womb], would, in most instances, amount to sheer speculation. To allow such a recovery will not only create and greatly increase litigation but will open wide the door to conjectural and fictitious claims.

For each and all of these reasons, I dissent.

## QUESTIONS

1. This case raises the question of the extent to which changes in scientific knowledge should bring about changes in the law. Are judges in the position to evaluate the extent to which scientific knowledge has changed? What if scientists disagree on an issue before the court?

2. Is it really a "medical" question whether the fetus is part of the mother?

3. Does society owe any duties to a fetus? Does society have any duties to distant future generations? How can judges determine whether these duties have been discharged?

## Niederman v. Brodsky (1970)†

*This case is an illustration of how a court may reverse itself and overrule its prior decisions. In Niederman v. Brodsky the Supreme Court of Pennsylvania rejected the "impact rule." This was the prevailing doctrine in the state, and it barred a plaintiff from recovering damages for emotional distress caused by another party's negligence unless the plaintiff received some physical blow or impact. In the opinion excerpted below, the court is not deciding the merits of the case (whether the plaintiff can collect). It is dealing only with the question of whether the plaintiff has a cause of action.*

---

\* The proximate cause of an injury is the event, act, or omission that immediately causes (or fails to prevent) the injury; the injury is the "natural" outcome of the proximate cause and would not have occurred without it.

† 436 Pa. 401, 261 A.2d 84 (1970).

JUSTICE ROBERTS:

Appellant, Harry Niederman, alleges that on November 4, 1962, he was walking with his son at the corner of 15th and Market Streets in Philadelphia. At that time, appellant's complaint asserts, appellee was driving a motor vehicle in a reckless and negligent manner, as a result of which the automobile skidded onto the sidewalk and destroyed or struck down a fire hydrant, a litter pole and basket, a newsstand, and appellant's son, who at that time was standing next to appellant. Almost immediately after this destructive path was cut by appellee's car, appellant claims that he suffered severe chest pain and that upon examination in the hospital, where he was confined for five weeks, appellant was diagnosed to have sustained acute coronary insufficiency, coronary failure, angina pectoris, and possible myocardial infarction. Consequently, appellant sought recovery from appellee for both these severe disabilities and the accompanying shock and mental pain.

Appellant's complaint was reluctantly dismissed on preliminary objections for failing to state a cause of action under the "impact rule," which provides that there can be no recovery for the consequences of fright and shock negligently inflicted in the absence of contemporary impact. Appellant admitted that the careening automobile had never struck his person. . . .

Today we decide that on the record before us, appellant may go to trial and if he proves his allegations, recovery may be had from a negligent defendant, despite the fact that appellant's injuries arose in the absence of actual impact. . . . Were we to do otherwise, appellant and those who are severely injured in a like manner would be barred from recovery in our courts. But the gravity of appellant's injury and the inherent humanitarianism of our judicial process and its responsiveness to the current needs of justice dictate that appellant be afforded a *chance* to present his case to a jury and perhaps be compensated for the injury he has incurred. . . .

An analysis of the prior case law indicated that there have been three basic arguments which in the past would have defeated appellant. The first deals with medical science's difficulty in proving causation between the claimed damages and the alleged fright. The second involves the fear of fraudulent or exaggerated claims. Finally, there is the concern that such a rule will precipitate a veritable flood of litigation. [Citations omitted.]

The first objection has been variously stated but the quotation [which follows] is representative of some earlier judicial sentiments. "In most cases, it would be impossible for medical science to prove that these subjective symptoms could not possibly have resulted from or been aggravated or precipitated by fright or nervous tension or nervous shock or emotional disturbance or distress. Medical science, we repeat, *could not prove* that these could not have been caused or precipitated, or aggravated by defendant's alleged negligent act." Bosley v. Andrews, 393 Pa. at 168-69, 142 A.2d at 267 (emphasis supplied). While we agree that this might have been an appropriate conclusion because of the lack of sophistication in the medical field when the impact doctrine was first announced in 1888, it would presently be inappropriate for us to ignore all of the phenomenal advances medical science has achieved in the last eighty years. Today diseases of the heart, for example, are comprehended much more fully (to the extent that open heart surgery is almost an everday occurrence), and the effects of hyperemotional states of the human body no longer are shrouded in mystery or myth. . . .

The logical invalidity of this objection to medical proof can be demonstrated further by noting that the rule has *only* been applied where there is absolutely no impact whatever. Once there is even the slightest impact, it has been held that the plaintiff can recover for any damages which resulted from the accompanying fright, even though the impact *had no causal connection* with the fright-induced injuries. . . .

It appears completely inconsistent to argue that the medical profession is absolutely unable to establish a causal connection in the case where there is no impact at all, but that the slightest impact . . . suddenly bestows upon our medical colleagues the knowledge and facility to diagnose the causal connection between emotional states and physical injuries. It can easily be urged that recent advances in medical science have bestowed this ability upon physicians; but it is illogical to argue that the presence of some slight injury has accomplished the same effect!

Finally, even if we assume that a great deal of difficulty still remains in establishing the causal connection, this still does not represent sufficient reason to deny appellant an *opportunity* to prove his case to a jury. There is no reason to believe that the causal connection involved here is any more difficult for lawyers to prove or for judges or jurors to comprehend than many others which occur elsewhere in the law. . . .

The second major objection includes the fear of fictitious injuries and fraudulent claims. [Discussion omitted.]

The last argument urged by the proponents of the impact rule is that: "If we permitted recovery in a case such as this, our Courts would be swamped by a virtual avalanche of cases for damages for many situations and cases hitherto unrecoverable in Pennsylvania." Knaub v. Gotwalt, 422 Pa. 271, 220 A.2d at 647. However, it is our view that this argument is currently refuted on two grounds. First, it is not at all clear that the flood of litigation has occurred in states without the impact rule. . . .

Secondly, and more compelling than an academic debate over the apparent or real increases in the amount of litigation, is the fundamental concept of our judicial system that any such increase should not be determinative or relevant to the availability of a judicial forum for the adjudication of impartial individual rights. . . .

We place the responsibility exactly where it should be; not in denying relief to those who have been injured, *but* on the judicial machinery of the Commonwealth to fulfill its obligation to make itself available to litigants. Who is to say which class of aggrieved plaintiffs should be denied access to our courts because of speculation that the workload will be a burden? Certainly this Court is unwilling to allow such considerations to influence a determination whether a class of litigants will be denied or permitted to seek adjudication of its claims. . . .

We today choose to abandon the requirement of a physical impact as a precondition to recovery for damages proximately caused by the tort in only those cases like the one before us where the plaintiff was in personal danger of physical impact because of the direction of a negligent force against him and where plaintiff actually did fear the physical impact. Since appellant's complaint alleges facts which if proven will establish that the negligent force was aimed at him and put him in personal danger of physical impact, and that he actually did fear the force, this case must proceed to trial. . . .

## QUESTIONS

1. The court notes that the "impact rule" was applied only when there was no impact at all; but if just the slightest impact occurred, then the plaintiff could recover for emotional injuries suffered. The court thinks there is something "illogical" and "inconsistent" about this. What is the alleged "illogicality"? Does this mean it is also unfair?

2. The court states, "the gravity of appellant's injury and the inherent humanitarianism of our judicial process and its responsiveness to the current needs of justice dictate that appellant be afforded a *chance* to present his case to a jury and perhaps be compensated for the injury he has incurred." Does this mean anything more than that it would be unfair to deny the appellant a chance to bring his case before a jury?

# III

# *Precedent and Analogy*

In the last chapter, we saw that the types of arguments employed in legal reaasoning should be examined from two perspectives: the forms of argument and the kinds of reasons given. Judicial arguments, as we saw, are not restricted to any one form, and judges offer various kinds of reasons for the truth or correctness of the premises of their arguments (appeal to good sense, goal-oriented reasons, rights-oriented reasons, etc.). Judicial arguments also, often implicitly, involve "practical" arguments, some varieties of which were identified. This chapter will concentrate on "appeal to precedent" and the role that arguments from analogy play in the use of precedents in legal reasoning. Before we turn to this subject, a few words should be said about the importance of the topic and about the limits of its treatment here.

It is perhaps sheer platitude to say that the courts play a central part in the development of the law. This is fairly obvious in the instance of constitutional law, in which a large body of law has been evolved through interpretations given by the Supreme Court to the relatively small number of words that make up the Constitution. Statutory law is law enacted by Congress or the state legislatures. It is plain that anyone who wishes to know the governing statutory law on a subject will have to give careful study to the way in which the courts have interpreted the statutes in question. But though much law is codified in the form of enacted statutes, a good deal of Anglo-American law is "case law"—law that has been developed by the courts in the decision of specific cases that have come before them. In an entirely non-controversial sense, case law is judge-made law. It would be impossible to speak of case law if judges did not in general follow the precedents established by prior courts in the deciding of cases. The principle that precedent should be followed is designated in the Anglo-American system by the Latin term *stare decisis,* an abbreviation of the phrase *stare decisis et non quieta movere* (to stand by what has been decided and not to disturb settled points).

## Adherence to Precedent

Why should prior decisions be followed?[1] First of all, according to a philosophical tradition that goes back to Aristotle, justice or fairness requires that like cases should be treated alike.[2] The principle of following precedent is somewhat analogous to Immanuel Kant's supreme moral principle, the categorical imperative: "Act only on that maxim through which you can, at the same time, will that it should become a universal law."[3] This moral principle rests in part on two sound intuitions: that a person cannot claim a right to perform a certain act unless he or she is willing to concede the same right to all other similarly situated persons, and that an act which is right (or wrong) to perform in a given situation is also right (or wrong) in all relevantly similar circumstances. Unless some explanation can be provided, one tends to think that a person who makes exceptions in favor of himself or herself, or who makes inconsistent moral judgments, is morally unprincipled. In a legal case, the losing litigants surely have good cause for complaint if the judge has rendered a precisely opposite decision in a prior case that was in no way significantly different from their own.

But the idea that like cases should be treated alike is a purely *formal* requirement of justice. It does not indicate what the substantively just treatment of a case would be, anymore than the two moral intuitions indicate what one has a right (no right) to do or what acts are right (or wrong). Neither does adherence to precedent guarantee substantive justice. In fact it has been criticized for having the opposite effect. "It is a maxim among . . . lawyers," says Gulliver, "that whatever hath been done before may legally be done again: and therefore they take special care to record all the decisions formerly made against common justice and the general reason of mankind. These, under the name of precedents, they produce as authorities to justify

---

[1] See also the discussion of principled decision, p. 64.
[2] Aristotle, *Nicomachean Ethics,* Book V. For an important recent discussion, see Ch. Perelman, *The Idea of Justice and the Problem of Argument* (New York: Humanities Press, 1963), Chapter 1.
[3] Immanuel Kant, *Groundwork of the Metaphysics of Morals,* Chapter 2.

the most iniquitous opinions; and the judges never fail of directing accordingly."[4]

Nevertheless, just as following the above moral intuitions helps to reduce subjectivity and bias, so also does adherence to precedent help to reduce arbitrariness and partiality. Moreover, following precedent does does have a relationship to substantive justice. When a case has been decided in a certain way, and especially after a line of similar cases has been decided in a particular way, people reasonably acquire the expectation that their own cases, if similar to these others, will also be decided in the same way.[5] Departure from the precedents will frustrate this reasonable expectation, and frustration of reasonable expectations is substantively unfair.

These last remarks have a bearing on another reason as to why precedents should in general be followed. Standing by what has been decided promotes predictability and certainty in the law, which are advantageous insofar as they enable people to plan their activities better. If courts were frequently to depart from the precedents, planning one's activities would become more difficult, for judges would be bringing their adjudications "into the same class as a restricted railroad ticket, good for this day and train only," as Justice Roberts said in dissenting from a holding that overruled previous cases.[6] On the other hand, the words "in general" in the first sentence of this paragraph must be emphasized. The principle of following precedent is not a rigid doctrine. Not only are the rules that are embodied in prior decisions occasionally overruled (see, for example, *Niederman v. Brodsky*, in the materials for Chapter 2), but the way in which courts handle precedents allows for their extension to new subject matter and, as well, their restriction to a limited range. In the words of Roscoe Pound:

> The chief cause of the success of our common-law doctrine of precedents as a form of law is that it combines certainty and power of growth as no other doctrine has been able to do. Certainty is insured within reasonable limits in that the court proceeds by analogy of rules and doctrines in the traditional system and develops a principle for the cause before it according to known techniques. Growth is insured in that the limits of the principle are not fixed authoritatively once for all but are discovered gradually by a process of inclusion and exclusion as cases arise

---

[4] Jonathan Swift, *Gulliver's Travels*, IV, 5.

[5] Compare, however, the concurring opinion of Judge Jerome Frank in *Aero Spark Plug v. B.G. Co.*, in the materials for this chapter.

[6] *Smith v. Allwright*, 321 U.S. 649, 64 S. Ct. 757, at 768 (1944).

which bring out its practical workings and prove how far it may be made to do justice in its actual operation.[7]

In this chapter we shall be examining various aspects of the treatment of precedents in order to see how certainty and change in the law are both possible. This subject should be of great interest to the student of moral philosophy, since the principle of *stare decisis* reflects the requirement of justice that like cases should be treated alike and because of similarities between the institutions of morality and law.

The discussion so far has been concerned with ethical considerations that underlie the principle of following precedent. Some technical questions about the principle must now be raised. These questions are very complex and it will not be possible to treat them in detail. The first is: *Whose* prior decisions is a judge bound to follow?

A glance at *Niederman v. Brodsky* provides a partial answer to this question. In his opinion, Justice Roberts refers to the fact that the judge in the trial court "reluctantly" had dismissed Niederman's complaint because of the "impact rule." This rule was well established in the state of Pennsylvania, in whose jurisdiction the case had arisen, by the prior decisions of the Supreme Court of Pennsylvania. And, said the trial judge, "We are bound by the law as set forth by the Supreme Court." We can take this case as illustrating the general proposition that the lower courts in any given jurisdiction are bound by the precedents set in that jurisdiction by its highest appellate court. Although judges are in the habit of referring to the decisions of coequal courts in their jurisdiction—and even to the decisions of courts outside their jurisdiction—by the term "authorities," and they therefore may appeal to these decisions as precedents for their own decisions, none of these other decisions has the same authoritative weight as the decisions of the highest court of their own jurisdiction.

As far as the highest court itself is concerned, the issue is more difficult. Obviously, if the principle of *stare decisis* is to have any significance at all, and if the principle genuinely reflects the requirement of justice that like cases should be treated alike, the highest court of a jurisdiction (as much as any court whose prior decisions on some questions have not been overruled) must in general be bound by its own precedents. Yet the highest court does have greater freedom in regard to its own prior decisions than any court that is subordinate to it. In *Niederman,* the Supreme Court of Pennsylvania

---

[7] Roscoe Pound, *The Spirit of the Common Law* (Boston: Marshall Jones Company, 1921), p. 182.

departed from its prior decisions and overturned the "impact rule" for Pennsylvania. It is essential to note, however, that in so doing, the court felt compelled to *justify* its departure from precedent and offered a number of arguments in this direction.[8]

Implicit in the above discussion are roughly three kinds of "appeal to precedent": (1) an appeal by a subordinate court to the prior rulings of the higher courts of its jurisdiction, (2) an appeal by a court to the decisions of any other court besides its higher courts, and (3) an appeal by any court to its own prior rulings. When a court *openly* departs from a ruling which it takes to have some precedential value, it ordinarily will attempt to justify its departure by an argument. Our concern in this chapter, however, is not so much the explicit overruling (usually by the highest court of a jurisdiction) of a line of prior decisions as it is the extension of a precedent to new subject matter or its restriction to a narrow range. The technique of restricting a precedent to a narrow range enables a judge to depart, in a sense, from prior rulings without defying or (if he has the authority to do so) overturning them. It is in these two ways of dealing with precedents—extension and restriction—that arguments by analogy become especially important.

Assuming, then, that prior decisions do have binding force, of whatever degree, for a judge, exactly *what* is it in the prior decision that has this force? This is a difficult question, and it cannot be treated in detail here. The standard position is that a judge is not bound by everything that was stated in the opinion on the prior case but only by its *ratio decidendi*, the reason for deciding the case in the given way. But there is much debate on how to extract the *ratio decidendi* from an opinion.

A relatively simple, if somewhat simplistic, approach to this issue will be adopted here. We are concerned with cases that raise a question of law and, as a minimum, the *ratio decidendi*—the part of the opinion that is binding on a future court—is the judge's answer to the question of law that was posed. Usually, however, the "reason for deciding" will be a proposition that has broader coverage than the fact-situation that gave rise to the question of law. Thus in *Priestley v. Fowler* the court dealt with the issue of whether the master could be held liable to the butcher boy if an injury resulted from the negligence of another employee in failing to keep the delivery van in a proper state of repair and in seeing that it should not be overloaded.[9] Lord Abinger answered this question in the negative, and although he did not

---

[8] The English doctrine of precedent is said to be more rigid than the American doctrine. See Rupert Cross, *Precedent in English Law*, 3rd ed. (Oxford: Clarendon Press, 1977). This book contains much of interest on American practice.

[9] However, see the headnote to the case in the materials for Chapter 1.

specifically state a general rule of law as the basis for the decision, it is quite clear that he did think there was a general principle under which the case fell. This is shown by his reference to other types of employees besides butcher boys (chambermaids, cooks, upholsterers, etc.) and by his general talk about masters and servants. And it is this general principle, however it is to be formulated, that constitutes the *ratio decidendi*. For the purpose of analyzing a case subsequent to *Priestley*, in which *Priestley* was regarded as an "authority," the "reason for deciding" would be whatever general principle or principles the later court took as the precedent that it should follow. A parallel approach will be adopted for the cases we shall analyze. Ordinarily, of course, the later court will view the precedent in the light of the argumentation and policy considerations given in the original opinion. So, for instance, some later judges cited *Priestley* as supporting the doctrine that employees voluntarily assume risks unless their contracts of employment provide otherwise.[10]

As stated earlier, we are interested in how judges expand and restrict the applicability of precedents, and the role that arguments by analogy play in this process. Later on it will be seen how the process works in a *line* of cases. But it is necessary, first, to look again at arguments by analogy.

## Argument by Analogy: Interpretations and Revision

Arguments by analogy involve the passage from assumed or given resemblances to an inferred resemblance. Thus, given that $x$ has characteristics F, G, and H and that $y$ has characteristics F and G, it is inferred that $y$ also has characteristic H. Now it is sometimes said the underlying basis of an argument by analogy is the following principle: If $x$ and $y$ have a number of characteristics in common, then any further characteristic found in $x$ will also be found in $y$. This principle, however, is clearly false, for in fact two things may resemble each other in any number of respects and yet also be different in any number of respects. What is necessary, in order to make the argument plausible, is the presumption that the characteristics in question are related to each other in a certain way, that possession of the given resemblances (F and G, in our example) is *relevant* to the possession of the inferred resemblance (H). (See the revised form of argument by analogy, p. 45.) Thus, in *Adams v. New Jersey Steamboat Co.* (pp. 46-47)

---

[10] *Priestley v. Fowler*, decided in 1837, was first cited in the United States in 1842, in *Farwell v. Boston & Worcester Railroad Corp.*, 4 Metc. (Mass.) 49 (railroad engineer injured as a result of switchman's negligence).

we saw, in effect, that (1) procuring a room for personal use and (2) having one's money and personal effects highly subject to fraud and plunder from one's proprietor are relevant to a proprietor's having a stringent responsibility, because these two characteristics are policy considerations for the law's imposition of this responsibility. Had Judge O'Brien found that a steamboat passenger is less subject to fraud and plunder from his proprietor than an inn guest, he might well have declined to find a stringent responsibility in the former instance.

Using the *Steamboat* case, let us consider a few of the ways in which judicial arguments by analogy may be interpreted. The first possibility is to conceive of the argument as actually involving two steps. The first step consists of *generalizing* a broad rule from the prior case(s). Since argument by analogy is an attempt to show something to hold of one case by appeal to a similar case, the judge should want this rule to cover both the prior case(s) and the new instant case. Let $D$ be the decision in a prior case. From $D$ the judge generalizes to the broad rule $R$, which also covers the facts of the instant case. The justification for $R$ would be an "appeal to the precedent" $D$. The second step consists in the *deduction* of the decision $D'$ for the instant case from $R$, since the instant case is subsumed under $R$. Under this interpretation there is, strictly speaking, no argument by analogy at all. Rather, the similarity between the cases functions to suggest, at the first step, the breadth or scope of the rule that is needed in order to get to $D'$. The weak point, so to speak, of the argument would be the first step of generalization.[11]

Although many judicial opinions can be interpreted in this way, especially since decisions should be principled, it seems doubtful that it literally describes the argument given in the *Steamboat* case. We would have to understand Judge O'Brien to be generalizing to the requisite broad rule from the innkeeper cases. What could that rule be? Perhaps the following: "All proprietors whose guests have procured (by payment) a room for personal use and who are in a position to defraud or plunder these guests are subject

---

[11] In his very valuable book *An Introduction to Legal Reasoning* (Chicago: University of Chicago Press, 1949), Edward H. Levi says: "The basic pattern of legal reasoning is reasoning by example. It is reasoning from case to case. It is a three-step process described by the doctrine of precedent in which a proposition descriptive of the first case is made into rule of law and then applied to a next similar situation. The steps are these: similarity is seen between cases; next the rule of law inherent in the first case is announced; then the rule of law is made applicable to the second case" (p. 1). It is not certain that by "rule of law inherent in the first case" Levi means a broad rule, like our $R$, which would cover both the previous and the new case, and that Levi's third step is deductive, as in the above interpretation. Some passages suggest this construal, but there are passages that suggest otherwise.

to a stringent responsibility toward them (i.e., proprietors are liable, without proof of negligence, for money stolen from their guests' rooms)." Given the premise "A steamboat proprietor is such a proprietor," the decision in the case follows deductively. Now the difficulty with this interpretation is that Judge O'Brien does not state any such broad rule and may well have hesitated to do so. Judges are sometimes leery of stating broader rules than they need. Still, it can be appropriate and useful to *reconstruct* an argument by analogy along these lines, for it may serve to make more apparent any implicit assumptions and any errors with respect to the acceptability of the premises.

A second possibility is to conceive of a judicial argument by analogy as concerned with a question of *classification*. This interpretation could plausibly fit the *Steamboat* case, for Judge O'Brien does speak of a steamboat as a "floating inn." The judge had the rule, established by prior cases, of the stringent responsibility of innkeepers. The question before him, then, would be whether a steamboat should, for certain legal purposes, be classified as an inn; and the conclusion that it should be is reached by his analogical argument. In a sense, no new rule about the liability of steamboat proprietors is needed because the case is subsumed under the original rule. This interpretation fits many arguments given in judicial opinions, and it raises an interesting philosophical issue.

Judges are often called on to answer classification questions that are put in the form "Is *X* a *Y*?" For instance: Is a golf club an inherently dangerous object? Is a bee a domesticated animal? Is a kiddie-car a vehicle? Is a fetus a person? What kind of questions are these? The form of the questions suggests that they are factual questions which have true or false answers, and to which the accumulation of factual information is germane in arriving at the true answers. On the other hand it has also been claimed that they are questions about the application of a name, to which any answer is arbitrary.

The philosopher John Wisdom has argued against these approaches:

> But the line between a question of fact and a question or decision as to the application of a name is not so simple as this way of putting things suggests. . . .
> In courts of law it sometimes happens that opposing counsel are agreed as to the facts and are not trying to settle a question of further facts, whether the man who admittedly had quarrelled with the deceased did or did not murder him, but are concerned with whether Mr. A, who admittedly handed his long-trusted clerk signed blank cheques did or did not exercise reasonable care, whether a ledger is or is not a document, whether a certain body was or was not a public authority.
> In such cases we notice that the process of argument is not a chain of demonstrative reasoning. It is a presenting and representing of those features of

the case which *severally cooperate* in favour of the conclusion, in favour of saying what the reasoner wishes said, in favour of calling the situation by the name
by which he wishes to call it. The reasons are like the legs of a chair, not the links
of a chain. Consequently although the discussion is *a priori* and the steps are not a
matter of experience, the procedure resembles scientific argument in that the
reasoning is not *vertically* extensive but *horizontally* extensive—it is a matter of
the cumulative effect of several independent premises, not of the repeated
transformation of one or two. And because the premises are severally inconclusive, the process of deciding the issue becomes a matter of weighing the
cumulative effects of one group of severally inconclusive items against the
cumulative effect of another group of severally inconclusive items, and thus lends
itself to description in terms of conflicting "probabilities." This encourages the
feeling that the issue is one of fact—that it is a matter of guessing from the
premises at a further fact, at what is to come. But this is a muddle. . . . The logic
of the dispute is not that of a chain of deductive reasoning as in a mathematic
calculation. But nor is it a matter of collecting from several inconclusive items of
information an expectation as to something further, as when a doctor from a patient's symptoms guesses at what is wrong, or a detective from many clues
guesses the criminal. It has its own sort of logic and its own sort of end—the solution of the question at issue is a decision, a ruling by the judge. But it is not an arbitrary decision though the rational connections are neither quite like those in vertical deductions nor like those in inductions in which from many signs we guess at
what is to come; and though the decision manifests itself in the application of a
name it is no more merely the application of a name than is the pinning on of a
medal merely the pinning on of a bit of metal. . . . With the judges' choice of a
name for the facts goes an attitude, and the declaration, the ruling, is an exclamation evincing that attitude. But *it is an exclamation which not only has a purpose
but also has a logic.* . . .[12]

Wisdom is making a number of claims. A classification question is not a
question of fact, and the answer is not the (more likely to be true than false)
conclusion of an inductive argument. Nor is it a question about the application of a name, to which any answer is arbitrary. The solution to such a
question is a decision, but not an arbitrary one. For it is a decision for which
reasons are given by pointing to the features of the items under discussion.
But although there is a reasoning process, the decision is not the conclusion
of a deductive argument. The process has "its own sort of logic." As applied to the *Steamboat* case, this would mean that Judge O'Brien's decision
was the "cumulative effect" of the similarity between the situations of inn-

keepers and steamboat proprietors—not just a psychological effect but presumably also a logical outcome of a unique sort. This approach to classification questions might be taken as a response to the issue posed in Chapter 2 (p. 48), whether it is appropriate to characterize judicial uses of analogical arguments in the same way as the other nondeductive arguments discussed earlier in that chapter. The objection was that in these other arguments the conclusion is, at most, shown to be more likely to be true than false, whereas the judge seems to presume to have established his result conclusively, as if it were the outcome of a formally valid deductive argument. According to the approach we have been considering, the conclusiveness of the judge's decision resides in his having *chosen* the result—not arbitrarily, but after a logically unique reasoning process. Under the interpretation of the *Steamboat* case as involving a classification question, this is how one should understand Judge O'Brien's conclusion that a steamboat is to be classified as an inn, especially since the judge saw "no good reason" for concluding (or choosing) otherwise.

There is a lot to be said about all this—although it is not easy to talk about what is supposed to be unique—but we can here consider only one point. Judges do deal with classification questions, but their form is easy to misconstrue. It is not simply "Is $X$ a $Y$?" but rather "Is $X$ a $Y$ for certain legal purposes?"—or better yet, "Should $X$ be treated as a $Y$ for certain legal purposes?" For instance, should bees be treated as domesticated animals for importation tax purposes? If one wishes to interpret the argument from analogy in the *Steamboat* case as being concerned with a classification question, one should view Judge O'Brien as asking whether steamboat proprietors should be treated as innkeepers for purposes of liability toward their passengers. (It may be clear that for some other purpose they should not be treated as innkeepers.) This way of putting the question has the advantage of revealing that the judge's affirmative answer is based on the claim that the same *practical* legal argument for imposing a stringent responsibility on innkeepers is also applicable to steamboat proprietors, because of the similarity between the two cases. If this construal is to be preferred, the above (Wisdomian) explanation of the conclusive character of the judge's classification decision seems to fail.

It would appear that the revised form of argument by analogy expounded in Chapter 2 (p. 45) ordinarily will be adequate to represent the analogical arguments used by judges and also how they handle classification questions, although the reasoning given in the opinions may need to be reformulated. Admittedly, there are cases of classification questions to which this pattern of argument does not fit. These occur when judges do not spell out the similarities (or differences) between the new case and the prior cases but simply assert their decision on the classification question because the similarities and differences seem obvious to them. But if the revised form of argument by analogy is ordinarily adequate, it still remains for us to explain the apparent conclusiveness of the judge's result, that is, to explain why a judge thinks his conclusion is not merely established as more likely to be true (or correct) than false (or incorrect). Let us proceed step by step.

It will be recalled, first, that legal arguments are normative arguments, in that they purport to establish how a case or class of cases *ought* to be treated (p. 42). Furthermore, these arguments are a species of practical reasoning (p. 55). A legal argument is supposed to provide a court with a reason for doing something, namely rendering a specific judgment. Now it is a characteristic of this context of practical normative reasoning that when a judge has a good reason for accepting a certain normative conclusion, he is *committed* to accepting and acting on the conclusion, unless there is (another) good reason for not doing so. This is a feature of practical rationality.

Let us now further revise the form of arguments by analogy. Consider the following:

(i)   $x$ has characteristics F, G . . .
(ii)  $y$ has characteristics F, G . . .
(iii) $x$ also has characteristic H.
(iv)  F, G . . . are H-relevant characteristics.
(v)   Therefore, unless there are countervailing considerations, $y$ has characteristic H.

This new revision has a *weaker* conclusion than the form on page 45. The weakness of the conclusion is brought out by the qualifying phrase "unless there are countervailing considerations," which is meant to reflect the point made in the preceding paragraph. In a nonnormative analogical argument of this form, which has descriptive premises and a descriptive conclusion, it would still be said that the premises do not logically entail the conclusion (the premises could be true while the conclusion is false), although whether this is the case may depend on how (iv) is interpreted and on what the qualifying phrase would mean in the particular context. But in a legal analogical argument, which is normative and practical, it is plausible to hold that the conclusion (v) is, in a sense, "entailed" by the premises: that is, that the truth (or correctness) of the premises commits a judge to accepting the conclusion.

It certainly seems to be the case that if there is a good reason for accepting a particular normative conclusion and no reason at all for not accepting it—which would be to interpret the qualifying phrase in the weakest possible way—then the conclusion ought to be accepted too. And one can go further: if there is a good reason for the conclusion and no good reason for not accepting it—which is how we shall interpret the qualifying phrase—then the conclusion ought to be accepted. If, then, a judge was to accept the premises of an analogical argument and was to draw the qualified conclusion (v), it is not difficult to see why he might consider the result as conclusively established. Let us look at the situation in a bit more detail.

Suppose a judge gives an argument by analogy of precedent, which heading we will take to include analogical arguments that use well-entrenched rules of the common (case) law.[13] In such an argument, for which the letters in the above form would be substituted by appropriate terms, premises (i) and (ii) ordinarily will be descriptive statements and their truth will be certified by appeal to the facts. Premise (iii), however, will be a normative statement, and its truth or correctness will generally be established by an appeal to a prior decision or trend of decisions. Thus in the *Steamboat* case, Judge O'Brien's premise (iii) was the proposition about the stringent responsibility of innkeepers (p. 47), which he took to be a settled rule of the common law, repeatedly affirmed in prior cases. Premise (iv) also will be a normative statement, and its truth or correctness may be established by an appeal to the precedent that is appealed to in reference to premise (iii).

Sometimes, however, judges omit their premise (iv), and they go directly from premises (i), (ii), and (iii) to an *unqualified* conclusion ("Therefore, *y* has characteristic H"). In other words, judges sometimes give arguments that have the form originally given for arguments by analogy (see p. 45). Nevertheless, we must assume that these judges are implicitly, if not explicitly, using a premise like (iv), and we should reconstruct their arguments accordingly. For the mere fact that their case resembles a prior case in some respects is never sufficient grounds for saying that their case also has the desired legal resemblance (H). There will always be some resemblances holding between their case and any number of cases of many different varieties. It has been said, in fact, that any two cases resemble each other in

---

[13] Arguments by analogy of statute and the use of analogical arguments in criminal law raise problems that cannot be considered here.

some respects. But since only relevant resemblances count, one is entitled to reconstruct a judge's analogical argument as including premise (iv).[14] In an argument by analogy of precedent in which the judge appeals to the *ratio decidendi* of a prior case, the presence of premise (iv) will be very close to the surface of the argument if it is not entirely explicit.

Before proceeding to the issue of the unqualified conclusion, two other aspects of premise (iv) should be noted. First, judges who give an argument by analogy of precedent surely will want their premises to add up to a good reason for accepting their conclusion. It was pointed out in the previous chapter (p. 56) that truth or correctness is one of the important criteria for something to be a good reason. But clearly, the truth or correctness of the premises is insufficient in this kind of argument for them to add up to a good reason; they must also be *relevant* to the conclusion. The relevance of premises (i), (ii), and (iii) is established through the relevance premise, namely, premise (iv). Again, then, if (iv) is omitted in a judge's analogical argument, one is justified in including it in one's reconstruction. The truth (or correctness) and relevance of the premises seem jointly sufficient to constitute the premises as a good reason for accepting (the qualified) conclusion (v).

Second, given the significance of premise (iv), it could be said that premise (iv) is "doing all the work," as it were. There is some truth to this remark, although premises (i), (ii), and (iii) are certainly indispensable to the argument. And there is a further important point. As stated earlier, in an argument by analogy of precedent, judges might establish their appropriate premise (iv) by reference to the prior case(s) on which they are relying with respect to premise (iii). But they might also try to establish premise (iv) independently, especially if they think there is a better rationale for it than the one in the prior case(s). In either event, however, the truth or correctness of premise (iv) will rest, in a more fundamental way, on underlying considerations of policy or principle. That is to say, the premise will generally rest on practical reasoning of the sort identified in Chapter 2—for example, goal-oriented or rights-oriented arguments. When judges extend a precedent to cover a new kind of case, as Judge O'Brien did in the *Steamboat* case, they should be understood as implicitly, if not explicitly, endorsing some underlying practical argument—perhaps the one of their precedential case(s).

It is not difficult to see why a judge can be justified in drawing the

---

[14] Any two cases will also differ from each other in some respects. But again, in *distinguishing* the instant case from a prior case, only relevant differences count.

weakened conclusion (v) from the premises (assuming them all to be true) in an argument by analogy of precedent. But, of course, he will want to draw a stronger conclusion, that is, an unqualified conclusion, which is the decision on the question of law. One possibility is to regard the judge as, in effect, subjoining an additional argument, using (v) as a premise:

> (v)   Unless there are countervailing considerations,
>        $y$ has characteristic H.
> (vi)   There are no countervailing considerations.
> _____
> (vii)  Therefore, $y$ has characteristic H.[15]

Given the truth (or correctness) of premise (vi), the judge's unqualified conclusion follows. Judges sometimes do explicitly affirm a premise like (vi). It will be recalled that Judge O'Brien saw "no good reason" for not applying the innkeeper rule to steamboat proprietors.

On the other hand, countervailing considerations often do present themselves. One way they arise is through a *competing analogy*. Insofar as arguments by analogy of precedent are concerned with classification questions, a competing analogy would suggest a different way of classifying the material facts of the case before the judge and would imply a different result, as shown by a parallel argument:

> (i′)   $z$ has characteristics J, K . . .
> (ii′)  $y$ has characteristics J, K . . .
> (iii′) $z$ also has characteristic non-H.
> (iv′)  J, K . . . are non-H-relevant characteristics.
> (v′)   Therefore, unless there are countervailing
>        considerations, $y$ has characteristic non-H.

In a legal system, premises (i)-(iv) could all be true (or correct) and so could premises (i′)-(iv′). In a sense, then, both conclusion, (v) and (v′), could also be true (or correct), for they do not contradict each other. What should a judge do in such an event? More generally, what should a judge do if there are countervailing considerations? The standard position is that the judge should *weigh* the considerations on each side, but there are no rules for how this weighing is to be done.

_____

[15] Compare Thomas D. Perry, *Moral Reasoning and Truth* (Oxford: Clarendon Press, 1976), Appendix III.

This problem takes us back to premises (iv) and (iv'). These premises rest on underlying considerations of policy or principle, expressed, for instance, in goal-oriented or rights-oriented arguments. If, as usually will be the case, premise (iv) rests on a different goal or right than premise (iv'), the judge should estimate which goal or right is the more important goal or right; the more important one is the weightier one. This estimate may or may not have "backing" in the authoritative sources, but it is hard to see how a judge can avoid making such an estimate in these circumstances; its deeper roots may lie in the judge's political philosophy and conception of the judicial role.

In view of the above remarks, the qualifying phrase should be reinterpreted to mean "unless there are countervailing considerations of equal importance." And (vi) should read: "There are no countervailing considerations of equal importance." Given the truth (or correctness) of premises (i)-(vi), a judge is justified in drawing the unqualified conclusion (vii). The fact that a judge might go immediately from premises (i)-(iv) to (vii) should be taken as an indication that he thinks there are no countervailing considerations of equal importance. It is, in fact, extremely difficult to find judicial opinions in which a judge who grants that there are good countervailing considerations to his conclusion also thinks that those considerations are as good as the reasons that support his decision.

Although a judge, in a given case, may believe premise (vi) to be true (or correct), he may not be able to claim to *know* it to be true (or correct). Premise (vi) might be disputed, and another judge sitting on the case may believe it to be false (or incorrect). So although conclusion (vii) is compelling for one judge, it need not be for another. It still can be said, however, that a judge who accepts premises (i)-(vi) is rationally committed to accepting conclusion (vii).

If this statement is right, one can understand why judges presume that the conclusions of legal arguments by analogy are not merely established as more likely to be true or correct than false or incorrect. The explanation of this presumption depends, as we have seen, on the fact that these arguments are normative and a species of practical argument. There thus appears to be at least one kind of good legal nondeductive argument that can conclusively establish its conclusion as true (or correct). One could, of course, treat such an argument as an enthymeme and turn it into a formally valid argument by supplying a missing premise (P): If (i), (ii), (iii), (iv), (v), (vi), then (vii). But there is no reason to regard (P) as true, unless one also agrees that this kind of nondeductive argument can conclusively establish its conclusion. (The analysis given here also applies to much of moral reasoning.)

## Case Law Development

Let us now study a few members from a *line* of cases that has often been used to show the technique of case law development.[16] The cases are from the Court of Appeals of New York, the highest court of the state. The line ends in 1916 with the scholarly majority opinion of Justice (then Judge) Cardozo in *MacPherson v. Buick Motor Co.*,[17] in which the prior cases are surveyed (see p. 41).

While riding in a car, MacPherson was injured as a result of the collapse of one of its wheels. The car was manufactured by the Buick Motor Company, which sold the car to a firm of automobile dealers, who in turn sold the car to MacPherson. The wheel was purchased by Buick, ready-made, from the Imperial Wheel Company, none of whose wheels had proved to be defective prior to the accident. The Buick Motor Company relied on the wheel manufacturer to make the necessary tests as to the strength of its wheels. The car was being prudently driven at the time of the accident and was going only eight miles an hour. MacPherson sued the Buick Motor Company for damages as a result of the injury. There was no claim that the company knew the wheel was defective when it sold the car to the dealer. The question in this case, as Judge Cardozo puts it, was whether the Buick Motor Company "owed a duty of care and vigilance to anyone but the immediate purchaser." Or as we may put it, did Buick in constructing the car also owe a duty of care and vigilance to MacPherson, the ultimate purchaser?

Some background is necessary in order to understand what is at issue. According to the old rule, which went back to the first half of the nineteenth century, a manufacturer, seller, or furnisher of an article was not liable to outside parties who had no contractual relations with him for negligence in the construction, manufacture, or sale of the article. In order to recover from the maker or supplier of a faultily made article, a party had to have a certain relationship to him, a relationship called "privity of contract." Thus the immediate purchaser might be able to recover for the failure to supply a properly constructed article; and if the immediate purchaser was proximately injured as a result of the negligent construction of the article he or she might also be able to recover damages—but no outside party could.

The leading authority in support of this rule was the 1842 English case

---

[16] For a fuller treatment, see Levi, *Introduction to Legal Reasoning*, pp. 1-19. The method of analysis and exposition employed here is somewhat different from Levi's, and the reader is urged to supplement this account with his.

[17] 217 N.Y. 382, 111 N.E. 1050 (1916).

*Winterbottom v. Wright.* Winterbottom, the driver of a mail coach, was injured when the coach upset on account of its defective construction. He sued Wright, who had an agreement with the postmaster general to provide the vehicle and keep it in repair. The court denied Winterbottom a right of recovery for the injury because there was no privity of contract between him and the coach provider. As the judge in the case, Lord Abinger, said: "If the plaintiff can sue, every passenger or even any person passing along the road, who was injured by the upsetting of the coach, might bring a similar action. Unless we confine the operation of such contracts as this to the parties who enter into them, the most absurd and outrageous consequences, to which I can see no limit, would ensue."[18] It is the privity of contract rule that Cardozo was calling into question in *MacPherson v. Buick.* For according to the rule, a duty of care in making the item was owed only to a party with whom there was a requisite contractual relationship.

The fact is that the New York court had departed from this rule in a number of cases. Cardozo, who was a master at harmonizing his decisions with prior decisions by subtly expanding some precedents and distinguishing others, was able to find that Buick did owe a duty of care to MacPherson. We shall survey some of the cases cited by Cardozo and see how they build up toward his opinion in *MacPherson.*

## THOMAS v. WINCHESTER (1852)[19]

The first case cited by Cardozo is *Thomas v. Winchester,* which in 1852 introduced an important exception to the privity of contract rule. Winchester was engaged in the business of manufacturing and selling vegetable extracts for medicinal purposes. His agent put up a jar of extract of belladonna, which is a poison, but mislabeled it as extract of dandelion, which is a harmless medicine. The jar was sold to a druggist, Aspinwall, who in turn sold it to a druggist, Dr. Foord. Mrs. Thomas was sick, and her physician prescribed a dose of dandelion for her. Mr. Thomas purchased some contents of the mislabeled jar from Dr. Foord. After taking a small quantity, Mrs. Thomas became gravely ill. The Thomases brought an action to recover damages from Winchester because of his negligence in putting up and selling the jar of poison as extract of dandelion. Here is a portion of Chief Judge Ruggle's opinion:

---

[18] See the short story by James Reid Parker, *"The Most Outrageous Consequences,"* in the materials for this chapter.
[19] 6 N.Y. 397, (1852).

CHIEF JUDGE RUGGLES:

The case depends on . . . whether the defendant, being a remote vendor of the medicine, and there being no privity or connection between him and the plaintiffs, the action can be maintained.

If in labeling a poisonous drug with the name of a harmless medicine, for public market, no duty was violated by the defendant, excepting that which he owed to Aspinwall, his immediate vendee, in virtue of his contract of sale, this action cannot be maintained. If A. build a wagon and sell it to B., who sells it to C., and C. hires it to D., who in consequence of the gross negligence of A. in building the wagon is overturned and injured, D. cannot recover damages against A., the builder. A's obligation to build the wagon faithfully arises solely out of his contract with B. The public have nothing to do with it. Misfortune to third persons, not parties to the contract, would not be a natural and necessary consequence of the builder's negligence; and such negligence is not an act imminently dangerous to human life.

So, for the same reason, if a horse be defectively shod by a smith, and a person hiring the horse from the owner is thrown and injured in consequence of the smith's negligence in shoeing; the smith is not liable for the injury. The smith's duty in such case grows exclusively out of his contract with the owner of the horse; it was a duty which the smith owed to him alone, and to no one else. And although the injury to the rider may have happened in consequence of the negligence of the smith, the latter was not bound, either by his contract or by any considerations of public policy of safety, to respond for his breach of duty to any one except the person he contracted with. . . .

But the case in hand stands on a different ground. The defendant was a dealer in poisonous drugs. Gilbert was his agent in preparing them for market. The death or great bodily harm of some person was the natural and almost inevitable consequence of the sale of belladonna by means of the false label. . . .

. . . In the present case the sale of the poisonous article was made to a dealer in drugs, and not to a consumer. The injury therefore was not likely to fall on him, or on his vendee who was also a dealer; but much more likely to be visited on a remote purchaser as actually happened. The defendant's negligence put human life in imminent danger. Can it be said that there was no duty on the part of the defendant to avoid the creation of that danger by the exercise of greater caution? or that the exercise of that caution was a duty only to his immediate vendee, whose life was not endangered? The defendant's duty arose out of the nature of his business and the danger to others incident to its mismanagement. Nothing but mischief like that which actually happened could have been expected from sending the poison falsely labeled into the market; and the defendant is justly responsible for the probable consequence of the act. The duty of exercising caution in this respect did not arise out of the defendant's contract of sale to Aspinwall. The wrong done by the defendant was in putting the poison, mislabeled, into the hands of Aspinwall as an article of merchandise to be sold and afterwards used as the extract of dandelion, by some person then unknown . . . .

. . . [the] distinction is recognized between an act of negligence imminently dangerous to the lives of others, and one that is not so. In the former case, the party guilty of the negligence is liable to the party injured, whether there be a contract between them or not. . . .

A few points in Chief Judge Ruggles's opinion should be noted. Ruggles does not derive his ruling, that Winchester can be held liable, from a precedent that had been established by a prior decision of the New York Court of Appeals. Instead, he *distinguishes* his case from *Winterbottom v. Wright*, so as to restrict the applicability of the rule established by the latter. He then implicitly uses a *practical* argument to establish a new legal principle for his case. Let us see how this is done.

There is a significant difference between the cases, Ruggles maintains, because the mislabeling of a poison intended for sale is an "imminently dangerous" act, whereas the making of a defective coach (or horseshoe) is not. A second feature of the *Thomas* case is that the medicine was made for sale to a remote purchaser. The use of the contents of the jar by someone other than Aspinwall, the immediate purchaser, was foreseeable by Winchester. These two features of the case combine to make Winchester's mislabeling of the jar a negligent act in relation to Mrs. Thomas. Ruggles's implicit practical argument goes something like this (cf. p. 55):

The law ought to protect people from acts of negligence imminently
    dangerous to their lives.
Imposition of a duty to exercise care in the making of imminently
    dangerous things is a means to this protection.
Therefore, the law ought to impose such a duty.

Because Winchester violated this duty, he can be held responsible for the injury even though he had no contractual relationship with Mrs. Thomas that would have required him to supply her with a properly labeled jar of medicine.

It should be noted that Ruggles speaks in terms of acts that are imminently dangerous and put human life in imminent danger, rather than in terms of imminently dangerous things. Yet it seems clear that he has some such category of things in mind too. This, at least, is how later judges understood his opinion. Plainly, there is room for disagreement on what acts or things are imminently dangerous. Ruggles defines an imminent danger to exist when death or great bodily harm is a "natural and almost inevitable consequence."

*Thomas v. Winchester* is a good illustration of the flexibility of the case

law system. It introduced a new principle into the law. But how far would
the law go with the change? Let us look at another case cited by Cardozo.

## LOOP v. LITCHFIELD (1870)[20]

JUDGE HUNT:

A piece of machinery already made and on hand, having defects which
weaken it, is sold by the manufacturer to one who buys it for his own use. The
defects are pointed out to the purchaser and are fully understood by him. This
piece of machinery is used by the buyer for five years, and is then taken into the
possession of a neighbor, who uses it for his own purposes. While so in use, it
flies apart by reason of its original defects, and the person using it is killed. Is the
seller, upon this state of facts, liable to the representatives of the deceased party?
. . . Under the circumstances I have stated, does a liability exist, supposing that
the use was careful, and that it was by permission of the owner of the machine?

To maintain this liability, the appellants rely upon the case of Thomas v.
Winchester. . . .

The appellants recognize the principle of this decision, and seek to bring their
case within it, by asserting that the fly wheel in question was a dangerous instrument. Poison is a dangerous subject. Gunpowder is the same. A torpedo is a
dangerous instrument, as is a spring gun, a loaded rifle or the like. They are instruments and articles in their nature calculated to do injury to mankind, and
generally intended to accomplish that purpose. They are essentially, and in their
elements, instruments of danger. Not so, however, an iron wheel, a few feet in
diameter and a few inches in thickness although one part may be weaker than
another. If the article is abused by too long use, or by applying too much weight
or speed, an injury may occur, as it may from an ordinary carriage wheel, a
wagon axle, or the common chair in which we sit. There is scarcely an object in
art or nature, from which an injury may not occur under such circumstances. Yet
they are not in their nature sources of danger, nor can they, with any regard to the
accurate use of language, be called dangerous instruments. That an injury actually occurred by the breaking of a carriage axle, the failure of the carriage body,
the falling to pieces of a chair or sofa, or the bursting of a fly wheel, does not in
the least alter its character.

. . . The injury in [Thomas v. Winchester] was a natural result of the act. It
was just what was to have been expected from putting falsely labeled poisons in
the market, to be used by whomever should need the true articles. It was in its
nature an act imminently dangerous to the lives of others. Not so here. The
bursting of the wheel and the injury to human life was not the natural result or the
expected consequence of the manufacture and sale of the wheel. Every use of the
counterfeit medicines would be necessarily injurious, while this wheel was in fact
used with safety for five years.

[20] 42 N.Y. 351 (1870).

Judge Hunt refuses to bring his case under the principle of *Thomas*, for the cases are readily distinguishable. A poison is a "dangerous instrument" but a fly wheel is not. It is opinions like the one in *Loop v. Litchfield* that give rise to the impression that classification questions have the form "Is *X* a *Y*?" However, taking the form that earlier was said to be proper, it should in any event be noted that Hunt's question is not "Should a fly wheel be treated as a poison for purposes of a manufacturer's liability?" but rather "Should a fly wheel be treated as a dangerous instrument for these purposes?" Hunt has adopted Ruggles's "imminently dangerous" thing as a legal category, and he gives examples of dangerous instruments: poison, gunpowder, a torpedo, etc. These things are in their nature calculated to do injury and hence are dangerous instruments. But a chair, a sofa, and a flywheel—even if defectively made—are not imminently dangerous instruments. One may expect Hunt's examples to pose a problem for later judges who might wish to extend the principle of *Thomas v. Winchester*.

As an exercise, let us see how Judge Hunt might have argued had he wanted to apply the precedent of *Thomas* to his case. He could have used an argument by analogy:

(i)   A manufacturer of medicines is a furnisher of a product whose use by someone other than the immediate purchaser may be foreseen and a furnisher of a product that is imminently dangerous if it is defectively made.

(ii)  A manufacturer of fly wheels is a furnisher of a product whose use by someone other than the immediate purchaser may be foreseen and a furnisher of a product that is imminently dangerous if it is defectively made.

(iii) A manufacturer of medicines is someone who owes a duty of care to the user in making the product.

(iv)  Being a furnisher of a product whose use by someone other than the immediate purchaser may be foreseen and being a furnisher of a product that is imminently dangerous if it is defectively made are relevant to owing a duty of care to the user in making the product.

(v)   Therefore, unless there are countervailing considerations, a manufacturer of fly wheels is someone who owes a duty of care to the user in making the product.

Of course, Hunt is not forced to this conclusion, because he rejects premise (ii); a fly wheel, he maintains, is not to be included in the category of imminently dangerous instruments. At any rate, this fly wheel was used with safety for five years. The precedent set by *Thomas v. Winchester* is not applicable, and manufacturers of many types of things can be fairly certain that they will not be liable to the consumer should injury result from a defectively made product.

## DEVLIN v. SMITH (1882)[21]

An 1882 decision in the Court of Appeals, *Devlin v. Smith,* might have given these people some pause. Smith was a painting contractor who entered into an agreement to paint the inside of the dome of the Kings County courthouse. He made a contract with Stevenson to build a "first-class" ninety-foot scaffold. Devlin, Smith's employee, was working on the curve of the dome when a ledger of the scaffold gave way. Devlin fell to the floor, and died of his injury. Devlin's family sued Smith and Stevenson. Here is a portion of Judge Rapallo's opinion:

JUDGE RAPALLO:
    If any person was at fault in the matter it was the defendant Stevenson. It is contended, however, that even if through his negligence the scaffold was defec tive, he is not liable in this action because there was no privity between him and the deceased, and he owed no duty to the deceased, his obligation and duty being only to Smith, with whom he contracted.
    As a general rule the builder of a structure for another party, under a contract with him, or one who sells an article of his own manufacture, is not liable to an action by a third party who uses the same with the consent of the owner or purchaser, for injuries resulting from a defect therein, caused by negligence. The liability of the builder or manufacturer for such defects is, in general, only to the person with whom he contracted. But, notwithstanding this rule, liability to third parties has been held to exist when the defect is such as to render the article in itself imminently dangerous, and serious injury to any person using it is a natural and probable consequence of its use. . . . (Thomas v. Winchester, 6 N.Y. 397).
    Applying these tests to the question now before us, the solution is not difficult. Stevenson undertook to build a scaffold ninety feet in height, for the express purpose of enabling the workmen of Smith to stand upon it to paint the interior of the dome. Any defect or negligence in its construction, which should cause it to give way, would naturally result in these men being precipitated from that great height. A stronger case where misfortune to third persons not parties to the contract would be a natural and necessary consequence of the builder's negligence, can hardly be supposed, nor is it easy to imagine a more apt illustration of a case

where such negligence would be an act imminently dangerous to human life. These circumstances seem to us to bring the case fairly within the principle of Thomas v. Winchester.

It would be easy to cast Rapallo's argument in the form just given. For the words "fly wheels" one need only substitute "scaffolds" (or should it be "ninety-foot scaffolds"?). The important point, however, is the difference between the ways in which Hunt and Rapallo conceive the "imminently dangerous" category of *Thomas v. Winchester*. According to the former, this categeory includes only things that are "in their nature calculated to do injury to mankind, and generally intended to accomplish that purpose." According to the latter, an article is imminently dangerous if a "serious injury to any person using it is a natural and probable consequence of its use." Judge Cardozo says in *MacPherson* that *Loop v. Litchfield* suggests a "Narrow construction" of the rule of *Thomas v. Winchester* while *Devlin v. Smith* evinces a "more liberal spirit." (It should be mentioned that Rapallo hasn't found Stevenson liable for the injury or death but only liable to an action; it is still a question for a jury whether Stevenson in fact was negligent in constructing the scaffold.)

If the maker or furnisher of medicines or scaffolds now owes a duty of care to the potential user, what is the status of manufacturers of, say, chairs or sofas, to refer to Hunt's examples? On the basis of *Devlin v. Smith* it is still possible that these manufacturers do not have such a duty. For although someone could be seriously injured as a result of the collapse of a defectively made chair or sofa, it might still be said that serious injury to any person using one is *not* a natural and probable consequence of its use. But would this be right? What does "natural and probable consequence" mean, anyway?

Before finally turning to *MacPherson*, let us take a look at an extract from one more case cited by Judge Cardozo.

## TORGESEN v. SCHULTZ (1908)[22]

In *Torgesen v. Schultz*, the plaintiff, a domestic servant, lost an eye when a bottle of aerated water (commonly known as club soda or seltzer) exploded on a hot July evening in 1901. A druggist delivered two bottles of the aerated water to the plaintiff's employer's house. The plaintiff received the bottles and put them in a third-story room for several hours. (The outdoor temperature that day reached into the upper 90s and was still in the 90s that

[22] 192 N.Y. 156, 84 N.E. 956 (1908).

evening). Between 7 and 8 P.M., the plaintiff took the bottles to the base-
ment of the house. She placed them upright in a pan containing ice, so that
one side of each bottle was against the ice. As she turned away, one of the
bottles exploded.

Torgesen brought her suit against the bottler of the water (Schultz), who
had sold the bottles to the druggist. Her case was dismissed for lack of a
cause of action against the bottler. On appeal, the Court of Appeals of New
York faced the question of whether the manufacturer could be held liable
even though he had not directly sold the bottles to the plaintiff's employer.

Here is an excerpt from the court's unanimous opinion, written by Judge
Willard Bartlett:

JUDGE WILLARD BARTLETT:
    To show the necessity of taking precautions to prevent such explosions, and
    also to show the extent of the precautions actually taken by the defendant to that
    end, plaintiff's counsel read in evidence certain extracts from a printed circular of
    the defendant, and counsel for the defendant also read certain other extracts . . .
    It is manifest that there was no contract relation between the plaintiff and the
    defendant, but the defendant is sought to be held liable under the doctrine of
    *Thomas v. Winchester* (6 N.Y. 397), and similar cases based upon the duty of the
    vendor of an article dangerous in its nature, or likely to become so in the course
    of the ordinary usage to be contemplated by the vendor, either to exercise due
    care to warn user of the danger or to take reasonable care to prevent the article
    sold from proving dangerous when subjected only to customary usage. . . .
    The language of the defendant's circular tends to show that it was well aware
    that siphons charged under pressure of 125 pounds to the square inch were liable
    to explode unless the bottles had been first subjected to an adequate test. This is
    plainly inferable from the statement: ''We take all possible precautions to guard
    against accidents.'' There could be no possible occasion for this assertion unless
    accidents were likely to happen in the absence of proper precaution to avert them.
    . . . The defendant might reasonably be held chargeable with knowledge that it
    was customary, especially in hot weather, to place siphons charged with aerated
    water in contact with ice, and in view of this fact a jury might well find that the
    tests applied to such bottles should be such as to render it tolerably certain that
    they would not explode when thus used. As has already been suggested, the ex-
    pert testimony indicated that the test actually employed by the defendant was not
    adequate to justify such a conclusion.
    It may very well be that the defendant, if put to its proof on the subject, may
    establish the adequacy of its test and that nothing further can reasonably be re-
    quired to be done to assure the safety of those making use of their charged siphons
    as against explosions  of the character which injured the plaintiff, but upon the
    evidence as it stood at the close of her case I think there was enough to entitle the
    plaintiff to have the question of the defendant's negligence submitted to the jury.

Judge Willard Bartlett, too, appeals to the precedent of *Thomas v. Winchester* to establish that defendant Schultz, a supplier of bottles of aerated water, owes a duty of care to a potential user who did not stand in a contractual relationship to him. We can take this case as posing a classification question: "Should a siphon bottle be treated as an imminently dangerous thing for purposes of a manufacturer's (or furnisher's) liability?" Plainly Willard Bartlett has rejected the narrow interpretation of the precedent given by Judge Hunt. *Thomas* covers not only an article "dangerous in its nature", but also one that is "likely to become so in the course of the ordinary usage to be contemplated by the vendor." And it is reasonable to say that the defendant knew, or should have known, that the bottle would be used under the described circumstance. There is, therefore, a duty of care in putting up the bottles, which is owed to the potential user irrespective of contract.

*Torgesen v. Schultz*, then, also evinces the more liberal spirit that Cardozo talked about. In fact, it seems to go a bit further than the *Devlin* case in opening up the exceptions to the privity of contract rule. Perhaps, though, the status of manufacturers of chairs or sofas is still not entirely clear.

We are now ready for excerpts from Judge Cardozo's opinion written for the majority of the court, in *MacPherson*. Judge Cardozo begins with a review of the facts.

## MACPHERSON v. BUICK MOTOR CO. (1916)[23]

JUDGE CARDOZO:

The defendant is a manufacturer of automobiles. It sold an automobile to a retail dealer. The retail dealer resold to the plaintiff. While the plaintiff was in the car, it suddenly collapsed. He was thrown out and injured. One of the wheels was made of defective wood, and its spokes crumbled into fragments. The wheel was not made by the defendant; it was bought from another manufacturer. There is evidence, however, that its defects could have been discovered by reasonable inspection, and that inspection was omitted. There is no claim that the defendant knew of the defect and wilfully concealed it. . . . The charge is one, not of fraud, but of negligence. The question to be determined is whether the defendant owed a duty of care and vigilance to any one but the immediate purchaser.

The foundations of this branch of the law, at least in this state, were laid in *Thomas v. Winchester* (6 N.Y. 397). A poison was falsely labeled. The sale was made to a druggist, who in turn sold to a customer. The customer recovered damages from the seller who affixed the label. "The defendant's negligence," it was said, "put human life in imminent danger." A poison falsely labeled is likely to injure any one who gets it. Because the danger is to be foreseen, there is a duty to avoid the injury. . . .

*Thomas v. Winchester* became quickly a landmark of the law. In the application of its principle there may at times have been uncertainty or even error. There has never in this state been doubt or disavowal of the principle itself. The chief cases are well known, yet to recall some of them will be helpful. Loop v. Litchfield (42 N.Y. 351) is the earliest. It was the case of a defect in a small balance wheel used on a circular saw. The manufacturer pointed out the defect to the buyer, who wished a cheap article and was ready to assume the risk. The risk can hardly have been an imminent one, for the wheel lasted five years before it broke. In the meanwhile the buyer had made a lease of the machinery. It was held that the manufacturer was not answerable to the lessee. . . .

These early cases suggest a narrow construction of the rule. Later cases, however, evince a more liberal spirit. First in importance is Devlin v. Smith (89 N.Y. 470). The defendant, a contractor, built a scaffold for a painter. The painter's servants were injured. The contractor was held liable. He knew that the scaffold, if improperly constructed, was a most dangerous trap. He knew that it was to be used by the workmen. He was building it for that very purpose. Building it for their use, he owed them a duty, irrespective of his contract with their master, to build it with care.

From Devlin v. Smith we pass over intermediate cases and turn to the latest case in this court in which Thomas v. Winchester was followed. That case is Statler v. Ray Mfg. Co. (195 N.Y. 478, 480, 88 N.E. 1063). The defendant manufactured a large coffee urn. It was installed in a restaurant. When heated, the urn exploded and injured the plaintiff. We held that the manufacturer was liable. We said that the urn "was of such a character inherently that, when applied to the purposes for which it was designed, it was liable to become a source of great danger to many people if not carefully and properly constructed."

It may be that Devlin v. Smith and Statler v. Ray Mfg. Co. have extended the rule of Thomas v. Winchester. If so, this court is committed to the extension. The defendant argues that things imminently dangerous to life are poisons, explosives, deadly weapons—things whose normal function is to injure or destroy. But whatever the rule in Thomas v. Winchester may once have been, it has no longer that restricted meaning. A scaffold (Devlin v. Smith, *supra*) is not inherently a destructive instrument. It becomes destructive only if imperfectly constructed. A large coffee urn (Statler v. Ray Mfg. Co., *supra*) may have within itself, if negligently made, the potency of danger, yet no one thinks of it as an implement whose normal function is destruction. What is true of the coffee urn is equally true of bottles of aerated water (Torgesen v. Schultz, 192 N.Y. 156, 84 N.E. 956). . . .

We hold, then, that the principle of Thomas v. Winchester is not limited to poisons, explosives, and things of like nature, to things which in their normal operation are implements of destruction. If the nature of a thing is such that it is reasonably certain to place life and limb in peril when negligently made, it is then a thing of danger. Its nature gives warning of the consequences to be expected. If to the element of danger there is added knowledge that the thing will be used by persons other than the purchaser, and used without new tests, then irrespective of contract, the manufacturer of this thing of danger is under a duty to make it carefully. That is as far as we are required to go for the decision of this case. There must be knowledge of a danger, not merely possible, but probable. It is possible to use almost anything in a way that will make it dangerous if defective. That is not enough to charge the manufacturer with a duty independent of his contract. . . . There must also be knowledge that in the usual course of events the danger will be shared by others than the buyer. Such knowledge may often be inferred from the nature of the transaction. But it is possible that even knowledge of the danger and of the use will not always be enough. The proximity or remoteness of the relation is a factor to be considered. We are dealing now with the liability of the manufacturer of the finished product, who puts it on the market to be used without inspection by his customers. If he is negligent, where danger is to be foreseen, a liability will follow.

We have put aside the notion that the duty to safeguard life and limb, when the consequences of negligence may be foreseen, grows out of contract and nothing else. We have put the source of the obligation where it ought to be. We have put its source in law.

From this survey of the decisions, there thus emerges a definition of the duty of a manufacturer which enables us to measure this defendant's liability. Beyond all question, the nature of an automobile gives warning of probable danger if its construction is defective. This automobile was designed to go fifty miles an hour. Unless its wheels were sound and strong, injury was almost certain. It was as much a thing of danger as a defective engine for a railroad. The defendant knew the danger. It knew also that the car would be used by persons other than the buyer. This was apparent from its size; there were seats for three persons. It was apparent also from the fact that the buyer was a dealer in cars, who bought to resell. The maker of this car supplied it for the use of purchasers from the dealer just as plainly as the contractor in Devlin v. Smith supplied the scaffold for use by the servants of the owner. The dealer was indeed the one person of whom it might be said with some approach to certainty that by him the car would not be used. Yet the defendant would have us say that he was the one person whom it was under a legal duty to protect. The law does not lead us to so inconsequent a conclusion. Precedents drawn from the days of travel by stage coach do not fit the conditions of travel today. The principle that the danger must be imminent does not change, but the things subject to the principle do change. They are whatever the needs of life in a developing civilization require them to be. . . .

We think the defendant was not absolved from a duty of inspection because it bought the wheels from a reputable manufacturer. It was not merely a dealer in automobiles. It was a manufacturer of automobiles. It was responsible for the finished product. It was not at liberty to put the finished product on the market without subjecting the component parts to ordinary and simple tests. . . The obligation to inspect must vary with the nature of the thing to be inspected. The more probable the danger, the greater the need of caution.

There is no need for us to review in detail the argument given by Judge Cardozo. We can see how his decision is the outcome of the *trend* of cases beginning with *Thomas v. Winchester.* But a few important points should be noted. It would be easy to cast Cardozo's argument in the form of the analogical argument that we supposed Judge Hunt might have given in *Loop.* For the term "fly wheels" we only need substitute "automobiles." As Cardozo says: "The principle that the danger must be imminent does not change, but the things subject to the principle do change." Yet, aside from the fact that the principle is no longer restricted to implements of destruction, is it so clear that the principle has not changed? In *Thomas,* Judge Ruggles defined "imminent danger" in terms of the "natural and almost inevitable consequence" of bodily harm; in *Devlin,* Judge Rapallo defined it in terms of the "natural and probable consequence" of injury; and in *Torgesen,* Judge Willard Bartlett allowed that "imminent danger" also covers what is "likely to become [dangerous] in the course of ordinary usage." It seems to me that Cardozo may be slightly extending the meaning of the term, although one could also say that he has merely clarified the meaning that is implicit in these definitions. For Cardozo, an "imminent danger" exists whenever injury is reasonably *foreseeable.* And, as he states in a part of the opinion not included in  the excerpt, "foresight of the consequences involves the creation of a duty." Since the manufacturer of a defective car can (or should) reasonably foresee injury to other people besides the immediate purchaser, he owes them a duty of care.

An interesting feature of Cardozo's decision is that it seems to be a complete reversal of *Winterbottom v. Wright,* to which *Thomas v. Winchester* was introduced as an exception.[24] *Winterbottom* involved a vehicle and *MacPherson* involved a vehicle; the latter case found liability to an outside party, the former did not. But Cardozo's interpretation of the "imminent danger" notion, an interpretation that harmonizes the trend of decisions, helps to explain this reversal. Cardozo may be seen as implicitly using a practical argu-

---

[24] See the excerpt from Judge Willard Bartlett's dissent in *MacPherson,* in the materials for this chapter.

ment that is somewhat different from the one identified for Judge Ruggles in *Thomas*. It goes something like this:

The law ought to protect people from acts of negligence of which injury is a foreseeable result.

Imposition of a duty to exercise care in making things which in ordinary uses foreseeably will result in injury, if they are defectively made, is a means to this protection.

Therefore, the law ought to impose such a duty.

There is now a broad principle that governs a manufacturer's liability to a potential user of a product, and it appears that the exceptions to the privity of contract doctrine have virtually swallowed up the rule.

Where does *MacPherson* leave the manufacturer of chairs or sofas? It seems far less doubtful that such a manufacturer does have a duty to potential users to exercise care; much depends, of course, on what the manufacturer can (or should) foresee. Cardozo says that "precedents drawn from the days of travel by stagecoach do not fit the conditions of travel today." The significance of this statement is not merely directed at explaining his departure from *Winterbottom,* from law appropriate to horse-driven vehicles to law appropriate to motor-driven vehicles. Cardozo would seem to be pointing out that in an industrial civilization very few consumers deal directly with manufacturers in acquiring the things they need, and that these people should have the same protection from harm as immediate purchasers get.

The series of cases we have traced is a good instance—one among many—of the operation of the case law system. The doctrine of precedent and the employment of the technique of analogical argument enable the law to meet two societal demands, stability and change.

## MATERIALS

*James Reid Parker,*
*"The Most Outrageous*
*Consequences" (1940)**

*One of the most significant occurrences in twentieth-century tort law has been the development of the area of manufacturers' liability. This development involved a liberalization of the law so that today a person injured by a defective product can*

* From James Reid Parker, *"The Most Outrageous Consequences."* Copyright 1940 by James Reid Parker. First appeared in *The New Yorker,* 16 (August 10, 1940), pp. 17-19. Reprinted from the book *Attorney at Law* by permission of Doubleday & Company, Inc.

*usually sue the manufacturer. As we saw in Chapter 3, this formerly was not possible
unless the injured party had purchased the product directly from the manufacturer.
The following fictional story by James Reid Parker (1909-    ) is based on this
change in tort law. It provides a useful overview of the significance of the developing
law through the eyes of an attorney who must break the news to his client that the legal
evolution culminating in* MacPherson v. Buick Motor Co. *means that the client will
likely be held liable in a lawsuit.*

Mr. Devore almost never lost a client except through the regrettable but
inescapable eventuality—in his own restful phrase—of death. It was un-
thinkable that he should lose the Wolverine Commercial Car Corporation,
which presumably wasn't susceptible to death and whose affairs at the New
York end were as profitable to the law firm of Forbes, Hathaway, Bryan &
Devore as those of any business they looked after. And yet this very
catastrophe, Mr. Devore told himelf, might occur if he continued to suffer
reversals in court, as he had been doing lately. Suppose this latest difficulty,
*Drucker v. Wolverine Comm. Car Corp.,* a rather minor case in its own
way, proved to be the breaking point? Mr. Devore, who was about to go
over and have a scheduled talk with Mr. Hibben, Wolverine's vice-president
in charge of the New York office, was thoroughly downcast. There could be
no doubt that Drucker, a taxi-driver who had been driving a Wolverine-built
cab for the Sun-Lite system at the time of his accident, had a legal precedent
for action. In the State of New York, at least. It was really a horrible precedent, handed down by a judge for whom Mr. Devore entertained bitter
loathing, but in Mr. Hibben's eyes this would not excuse defeat, as Mr.
Devore knew very well.

Perhaps what grieved the old lawyer most was that his sympathies were
with Wolverine, for basically there was something about a Comm. Car
Corp. that appealed to him. He loved Wolverine. Nor was his devotion
altogether that of a pensioner; he felt toward Wolverine much as a dog might
feel toward a life-long, if at times unreasonable, master. Mr. Devore put on
his derby, selected Ames and Smith's "Law of Torts" from his bookcase,
and gloomily started for the Wolverine offices. His first job, clearly, was to
mollify Mr. Hibben, if such a thing could be accomplished.

Mr. Hibben greeted him with the barest civility and at once asked the
question that Mr. Devore least wanted to hear.

"Well, what chance have we got?"

Before replying, Mr. Devore seated himself very solemnly, although the
vice-president had not suggested that he do so, placed the tort collection on
the desk in an impressively deliberate manner, and tried to look as much as
possible like Mr. Chief Justice Stone on a Monday afternoon.

"The first thing we must consider," he said slowly, caressing the torts as if to put himself under the protection of all the great adjudicators of the past, "is the historic attitude of the courts toward liability."

Mr. Hibben failed to assume the attentive expression of one about to enjoy a scholarly excursion into legal history. "That's not answering my question," he said.

Recklessly, Mr. Devore evaded the issue. "When a somewhat similar case was decided in the Court of the Exchequer in 1842, our American courts lost no time in adopting the decision as a precedent for this country. I'm happy to say that it was a complete and triumphant vindication of the defendant."

"And you say America adopted the same law intact?" Mr. Hibben asked eagerly.

"America accepted the precedent," Mr. Devore acknowledged, wondering how on earth to proceed from this point. It had perhaps been bad strategy to appease Mr. Hibben at the very beginning. The vice-president was nodding with satisfaction and saying, "Fine! Good thing Americans knew enough to tell right from wrong in those days. They don't seem to any more." If Mr. Hibben would only refrain from asking whether the precedent had ever been set aside!

"Is this law still O.K.?" Mr. Hibben asked. "You're sure the judges all know about it?"

"Oh, yes, they all know about it," said Mr. Devore soothingly and with perfect truth. "The case that set the precedent was really very much like the Drucker affair. I'd like to tell you about it."

Mr. Hibben now seemed more disposed toward a little excursion into the annals of the Court of the Exchequer. He offered his counsellor a cigar.

"It involved a chattel-maker's liability, or to be more exact, a chattel vendor's liability, to a third person," said Mr. Devore, making a heroic effort to be elementary. "The defendant Wright had contracted to supply mailcoaches to the Postmaster General, who had in turn contracted with a man named Atkinson, and his business associates, for a regular supply of horses and coachmen. Atkinson engaged the plaintiff Winterbottom to drive a coach between Hartford and Holyhead. In other words, A contracted with B, who contracted with C, who contracted with D. One day, most unfortunately, Winterbottom's mailcoach broke down because of a latent defect in its manufacture and he became lamed for life. Seeking damages, D sued not C, his employer, nor B, the Postmaster General, but the original A, with whom D had entered into no contract of any sort whatever."

After digesting these complications, Mr. Hibben said, "If D was hired by C, I think C was the one D should have picked to sue."

Mr. Devore agreed that this would have been a more usual procedure, but added that A was probably a wealthier firm and therefore a more tempting victim against whom to secure a judgment. The analogy was at once apparent to Mr. Hibben, who grunted in a shocked manner. Matters were progressing smoothly at the moment, but it meant only temporary relief for Mr. Devore. Nevertheless, he opened his Ames and Smith with convincing equanimity and turned to *Winterbottom v. Wright.*

"I'm sure you'll agree with me that Lord Abinger, the Chief Baron, expressed the whole issue very satisfactorily when he said, "If the plaintiff can sue, every passenger, or even every person passing along the road, who was injured by the upsetting of the coach, might bring similar action. Unless we confine the operations of such contracts as this to the parties who entered into them, the most absurd and outrageous consequences, to which I can see no limit, would ensue."

"Exactly!" said Mr. Hibben. "That's almost word for word what I told our legal adviser in Flint when I talked to him on the phone several days ago. It looks as if you've found a loophole all right, Devore." Mr. Hibben beamed at him. "I've always said it wouldn't pay Wolverine to maintain a full-sized legal department when we've got Forbes, Hathaway to take care of us. Frankly, Devore, the fellows out in Flint have been a little disappointed with your work lately, but they'll be tickled to death about *this.*"

Mr. Devore tried to smile but wasn't quite able to manage it. Something told him that the fellows in Flint weren't going to do any elaborate rejoicing. And if Wolverine were suddenly to install a full-sized legal department, what would happen to Forbes, Hathaway, Bryan & Devore? What, especially, would happen to Devore?

"I certainly like what he says about confining the operations of such contracts," said Mr. Hibben. "Let's hear that part again."

"Unless we confine the operations of such contracts to the parties who entered into them?"

"That's it!" Mr. Hibben said. "That's telling 'em! Why, we never had any dealings at all with Drucker. What we did was sell a cab to the Sun-Lite people, and Drucker was hired by Sun-Lite. Furthermore, it was a defective steering column that broke, and we don't even make steering columns. We buy them from Collins & Kemper!"

His exuberance was a terrible spectacle to Mr. Devore, who didn't quite know how to cut it short.

"Every passer-by," Mr. Hibben said, "every Tom, Dick, and Harry under the sun would start suing. They'd say they were suffering from mental shock or something as a result of being on the scene when the accident happened. Who is this man Abinger, anyway? I'd like to meet him."

"You're forgetting when the case was decided," Mr. Devore reminded him gently. "It was decided back in 1842."

He turned to another section of his Ames and Smith and, marshalling such courage as he had left, prepared to explain why Wolverine, and not Sun-Lite, would be required by law to yield to the plaintiff.

"In recent years," he began, "the most malign forces imaginable have been at work in this country. They have penetrated our government and—much as I dislike confessing the fact—our bar and our bench as well." A look of surprise crossed Mr. Hibben's face. "You don't have to tell me that!" he snapped.

The unhappy counsellor not only had to tell him but had to tell him without any further postponement.

"You'd be amazed at something that happened once in the Court of Appeals right here in New York," Mr. Devore said lightly. "It was the really unusual case of MacPherson against the Buick Motor Company—I mean the old Buick company, not the General Motors subsidiary. What happened was that the manufacturer sold one of its cars to a retail dealer, who in turn sold it to this man MacPherson. While MacPherson was driving the car, one of the wheels suddenly collapsed. He was thrown out and injured. The wheel had been made of faulty wood. The wheel wasn't made by Buick; it was bought from another manufacturer, just as you buy your steering columns from Collins & Kemper. The Court decided there was evidence, however, that the defects could have been discovered by reasonable inspection, and that inspection was omitted."

"Certainly inspection was omitted," said Mr. Hibben. "They probably bought their wheels from a reputable firm, and they certainly couldn't go around inspecting hundreds of thousands of wheels just on the chance that maybe they'd find one that wasn't exactly uniform. Why, in our case the steering column on Drucker's cab was the first defective column we'd ever heard about."

"I rather imagined that you'd see a similarity between the Drucker case and MacPherson against Buick."

"Of course I see a similarity," said Mr. Hibben.

Mr. Devore took a deep breath and jumped into the flames.

"I think you'll be interested in hearing what one of the judges said about it." The vice-president nodded, evidently retaining great faith in the book from which Mr. Devore had produced the fascinating mailcoach decision. "The judge held that 'if the nature of a thing is such that it is reasonably certain to place life and limb in peril when negligently made, it is then a thing of danger. Its nature gives warning of the consequences to be expected. If to the element of danger there is added knowledge that the thing will be used by persons other than the purchaser, and used without new tests, then, irrespective of contract, the manufacturer of this thing of danger is under a duty to make it carefully.''' He coughed nervously as he neared the most disagreeable part of the whole wretched decision. '''We are dealing now with the manufacturer of the finished product, who puts it on the market to be used without inspection by his customers. If he is negligent where danger is to be foreseen, a liability will follow.'''

"Wait a minute," said Mr. Hibben. "That line about 'the manufacturer of the finished product' would apply to Collins & Kemper. Drucker could sue *them* if he wanted to. Why don't you write him a letter and tell him about it?"

Mr. Devore shook his head and went on hastily.

"We think the defendant was not absolved from a duty of inspection because it bought the wheels from a reputable manufacturer." Here Mr. Hibben opened his mouth in horrified astonishment but made no comment. "It was not merely a dealer in automobiles. It was a manufacturer of automobiles. It was responsible for the finished product. It was not at liberty to put the finished product on the market without subjecting the component parts to ordinary and simple tests."

"You mean to say he's blaming the automobile manufacturers even though it was someone else who made the defective wheel?" asked Mr. Hibben. "You mean they'd be just as likely to blame *us*?"

But Mr. Devore, now that his great step had been taken, was unable to stop reading. "'The defendant knew the danger. It knew also that the car would be used by persons other than the buyer.'"

"Why, it might be a *child* talking," Mr. Hibben gasped.

"'Precedents drawn from the days of travel by stagecoach do not fit the conditions of travel today,'" Mr. Devore quoted, reading as quickly as possible. "'The principle that the danger must be imminent does not change, but the things subject to the principle do change. They are whatever the needs of life in a developing civilization require them to be.'" He closed the book with an abrupt gesture. His own patience had worn quite as thin as the vice-president's.

There was a long silence before Mr. Hibben said wearily, "Where did you say this terrible thing happened? Here in New York?"

"Yes. In 1916."

"Couldn't we take it to the Supreme Court? They may have *some* sense of honor and decency left."

Mr. Devore lighted one of his own cigars and closed his eyes. "That opinion was written by Benjamin Cardozo. No court in the United States would reverse a Cardozo ruling, even if it wanted to. Not in times like these."

"I see what you mean," murmured the vice-president. "Good God!" There was infinite worry in the way he spoke the words.

"Well, there you are, Hibben," said Mr. Devore presently. He waited for the storm to break. And then, even as he waited, the realization came to him that everything was going to be all right. It had been Cardozo, and not he, who had jumped into the flames. If Mr. Hibben entertained any feeling toward him, it was the sympathetic feeling that the same malign forces were in league against them both. Wolverine still loved him, and if he played his cards carefully, it would continue to do so. He leaned back and for the first time really tasted the flavor of his cigar.

## Jerome Frank,
## The Role of Precedent (1942)*

Aero Spark Plug Co. v. B. G. Co. *involved a claim of patent infringement. In a concurring opinion, Judge Jerome Frank took the time to deal with the role and significance of precedent in judicial decision making. He discussed the reasons for, and limits to, standing by precedent. This excerpt should be examined in relation to the justification of the principle of following precedent, as the justification is presented in the text (pp. 97-98). (On Frank, see the headnote on page 11.)*

JUDGE FRANK, concurring.

. . . Perhaps the central theme in most discussions of the judicial process is the obligation of judges to consider the future consequences of their specific decisions. Such discussions, usually stress the "rule" or precedent aspect of decisions. Thus Dickinson, in 1927, paraphrasing (it may be unconsciously) Aristotle's remarks made almost twenty-two hundred years earlier, writes, "One danger in the administration of justice is that the necessities of the future and the interest of parties not before the court may be sacrificed in favor of present litigants"; he thinks it imperative that judges should "raise their minds above the immediate case before them and subordinate their feelings and impressions to a practice of intricate abstract reasoning, . . . centering their attention on a mass of considerations which lie outside the color of the case at bar."

Although much can be said for that attitude—of considering a decision primarily with referrence to its significance in future cases—it is sometimes given too much weight. Excessive concentration of attention, by some upper court judges, on the formulation in their opinions of so-called legal rules,

* 130 F.2d 290, 294-99 (1942).

with an eye chiefly to the impact of those rules on hypothetical future cases not yet before the court, sometimes results in their allotting inadequate attention to the interests of the actual parties in the specific existing cases which it is the duty of courts to decide. Such judges never quite catch up with themselves; for, in cases which actually occur, they are deciding future cases that may never occur. Legal history shows that such an attitude leads to judicial pronouncements which, at times, are none too happy in their effects on future cases. For the future develops unanticipated happenings; moreover, it does not stay put, it refuses to be trapped.

The intended consequences of efforts to govern the future often fail; the actual consequences—which may be good or evil—are, frequently, utterly different. Results are miscalculated; there is an "illusion of purpose." . . .

And the paradox is that when judges become unduly interested in the future consequences of their rulings, they are (as Walter Bingham pointed out years ago) doing precisely what they say they must avoid—they are deciding not real but hypothetical cases, with no one present to speak for the imaginary contestants. The interests of the parties to cases actually before the court are thus sacrificed to the shadowy unvoiced claims of suppositious litigants in future litigation which may never arise; and the judicial process becomes the pursuit of an elusive horizon which is never reached. No one—except perhaps those judges—is satisfied, since the interests of the parties to real present cases are overlooked, and the interests of the parties in subsequent cases are often inadequately determined in their absence. No doubt it expands the ego of a judge to look upon himself as the guardian of the general future. But his more humble yet more important and immediate task is to decide individual, actual, present cases. The exaggerated respect paid today to upper court judges, as distinguished from trial court judges, is both a cause and a result of this over-emphasis on the rule-aspect of decisions. . . .

The elaborate (and sometimes fatuous) concern with the future potentialities of expressions in judicial opinions, which accompany and justify specific decisions is, in considerable measure, due to uncritical veneration of the doctrine of "standing by the precedents"; for, if an opinion does, in truth, lay down rules which must thereafter be followed by the courts themselves in later cases, the responsibility in deciding existing controversies is far greater than that of being fair to the parties to those controversies, for then a judge is playing the important role of legislator. That responsibility, however, can be too much underscored.

*Stare decisis*, within limits, has undeniable worth. As we said recently, "Of course, courts should be exceedingly cautious in disturbing (at least retrospectively) precedents in reliance on which men may have importantly changed their positions." As I have said elsewhere, "undeniably, in order to achieve impartial administration of justice, 'equality before the law,' and legal certainty, as far as is practicable, it is important, generally, that a court should not deviate, except prospectively, from its own decision in a prior case, even if that decision was in error, especially where such deviation will harm persons who acted in reliance upon that decision—as, for instance, a decision assigning specific legal consequences to specific words in a deed or lease." But precedent-worship has been so unreflective that there has been insufficient inquiry into its practical workings. . . . We have paid too little heed to the way in which John Chipman Gray—a successful practicing lawyer in the field of real property where, above all, precedent has been traditionally sanctified—challenged the fundamental thesis of *stare decisis* when he said that few men, in the conduct of their practical affairs, actually rely on past judicial rulings. Perhaps his scepticism went too far. Yet, in the twenty years which have elapsed since he issued that challenge few persons have met it, and most lawyers and many judges go on declaiming that life would be unbearably uncertain if courts did not adhere to their earlier formulations of "rules" and "principles." We know virtually nothing of the extent to which men do, in fact, rely on past judicial utterances. . . . [I]f the sanctity of *stare decisis* were thus moderately diminished, and if authorities were employed as they were by the much abused scholastics, i.e., only when shown to be reasonable, upper court judges might lose some of their prestige, but they could, by reducing their Jovian aloofness, devote more time to the interests of litigants in specific actual cases and less to the possible future harm of "just" decisions of those actual controversies.

## QUESTION

1. One reason for "standing by precedents" is that justice requires like cases to be treated alike. Did Frank reject that notion in this opinion?

## Felix S. Cohen, "The World-Line of a Precedent," (1950)*

*Felix Cohen (1907-1953) was a philosopher and lawyer. His father (Morris) was also a distinguished legal philosopher. For fourteen years Cohen served as a lawyer with the Department of the Interior. His specialty was in the field of American Indian Law. After leaving the federal government, Cohen taught at the Yale Law School and maintained a*

* Felix S. Cohen, *"Field Theory and Judicial Logic,"* Yale Law Journal, 59 (1950), pp. 238, 244-249. Reprinted by permission of the Yale Law Journal Company and Fred B. Rothman & Company from *The Yale Law Journals.*

*private practice. He frequently wrote on the relationship between law and ethics, and on the logical nature of legal questions and propositions. He is identified as a member of the legal realist movement. In the following excerpt from a 1950 law review article, Cohen examines the role of precedent in judicial reasoning. He compares precedent development with the scientific concept of field theory. He argues that just as a particle moving through a field has its course altered by the field, so a line of legal decisions has its course of development altered by the judges who deal with it. Cohen believes this happens because judges have different values and filter case precedents through these values.*

*The reader should analyze the line of cases from Thomas v. Winchester to MacPherson v. Buick Motor Co. in the light of this selection. Consider, also, whether Cohen's account is consistent with the treatment of argument by analogy of precedent given in Chapter 3.*

The problem of judicial precedent has been a focus of legal philosophy in America for more than a generation. Those who have criticized our courts for obstructing the paths of progress have generally suggested that the chief trouble with our judges is that they pay too much attention to precedent. Perhaps a stronger case might be made for the conclusion that judges pay too little attention to precedent and, therefore, often misread the lessons of the past. . . .

The fact is, however, that the question whether courts should follow precedent as much as they do is a wholly misleading question. Conformity to history, as Justice Holmes observed, is only a necessity and not a duty. What is true of history in general is equally true of that part of legal history that we call judicial precedent. No judge could possibly hand down a decision in any case for which a commentator could not find a precedent, even if the judge himself failed to find one. To say that a decision is unprecedented is to say either (1) that we do not agree with the use it makes of the precedents, or (2) that we do not know the precedents that might be cited in its support. Each of these statements tells us a good deal about the person who makes the statement but very little about the nature of the decision and its relation to the past. In this respect, the statement that a decision is unprecedented is very much like the statement that certain philosophical or literary works are "original"; such allegations only measure the allegator's ignorance of history. In short, the real question is not *whether* judges should follow precedent (or logic or the law of gravitation or anything else that they cannot help following, whether they know it or not). It is, rather, *how* they should follow precedent, that is, how they should interpret past cases and how they should draw the lines of similarity that connect past cases and present cases.

One of the unfortunate consequences of the sustained controversy over the judicial duty to follow or to ignore precedent in the interest of social welfare is the impression that following precedents is a process of logic. "Up with logic" and "Down with logic" have become the battle slogans in a controversy where logic is essentially neutral, as it is in all human controversies. Actually, logic can never establish that one case is a precedent for another case. That is because no two cases can possibly be alike in all respects. (If they were alike in all respects, then, according to the principle of the identity of indiscernibles, they would be one case, not two cases.) Any two cases, however selected, are alike in some respects. (Otherwise, they would not both be "cases.") Whether the respects in which two cases are alike are important is a question not of logic but of values. Within one framework of values, it makes no difference whether the defendant in a damage suit is a helpless widow, a powerful steel corporation, a person of Japanese ancestry during a war with Japan, a pugnacious labor leader, or a government official. Under such a standard of "impartiality," the differences between the parties become irrelevancies. But to a judge who thinks that differences between defendants ought to be given weight, and to a lawyer or observer who thinks that such differences are given weight, the differences between the parties in the earlier case and the pending case may seriously change or destroy the precedent-value of the earlier case. . . .

If significant differences between cases may flow even from differences in dates of decision and differences in the parties, the fact remains that further differences can always be found, as a practical matter, between any two cases. There is no precedent that cannot be distinguished away if you want to distinguish it. The use of a precedent always implies a value judgment, a judgment that similarities between the precedent and the following decision are important and that dissimilarities are relatively unimportant. The application of precedent thus always involves a process of selection or discrimination. But one man's pattern of selectivity is not the same as another man's. A judge who thinks that labor organization ought to be encouraged will rebel when decisions in antitrust cases involving capital are invoked against labor. . . .

According to the common view, it is logical to follow precedents but illogical to make precedents. But even slight acquaintance with the development of modern logic makes it clear that logic is no respecter of age. There is logic in change as well as in constancy. . . .

Disagreeing judges and opposing counsel will regularly disagree as to whether a precedent is squarely on point, not because either side is mistaken in its logical calculations but because the two sides bring to bear upon the issue different sets of value judgments. Ordinarily these value judgments are not made explicit. To make them explicit would, as Holmes has said, deprive judges of "the illusion of certainty which makes legal reasoning seem like mathematics." Often the judges who make these implicit value judgments are not aware of them and would bitterly and honestly resent the imputation that they are allowing their own value judgments to enter into the decision of cases. In this respect, again, judges are like other human beings. . . .

The selectivity operation that we execute when we hold up one decision as precedent for another decision will, in general, expand the force and scope of those decisions that we agree with; at the same time it will restrict the force and scope of decisions that we think wrong and ill-advised. In dealing with decisions that we approve of we will generally, consciously or unconsciously, stress the broad principles of justice enunciated in the case. The decision we disapprove of we may seek to restrict to "the facts of the case as it was actually decided," which is a politely circuitous way of saying that we would not give the decision any weight at all in any later case. But we do not have to go so far in order to free ourselves from the incubus of an apparent precedent. We are bound to find some points of difference [between any two cases]. . . .

. . . What is important to recognize is that the shape of a precedent, as well as it size, will vary with the selectivity-grid through which it is viewed. One side of the precedent may grow while the opposite side shrinks. And a series of cases which looks like a straight line from one value standpoint may look like a very crooked stick from another.

If these variations in the shape and force of a precedent were completely unpredictable, law would have all the uncertainty that Jerome Frank thought it had before he became judge. But the fact is that we do know something about the selectivity patterns of most judges which shape the line of development of any precedent. In fact a very important part of the process of selecting judges is devoted to the eliminating of judges with disrespectable or unpredictable value patterns. When we find a marked judicial shift in value judgments, as in Chief Justice Hughes' and Justice Roberts' opinions in the first Labor Board cases, we can tell that other precedents in many other fields of law will thenceforward cease to be precedents because a new value-attitude has been taken (though not expressly formulated) with respect to social legislation.

According to traditional judicial logic, every precedent moves in a straight line, imparting its direction to every case that gets in its way. In fact, however, we find that the force and direction of a precedent vary with the field in which it is observed. We are not now, and probably never will be, able to predict the path of a precedent with absolute certainty. No more can we always, with complete assurance, predict the path of a merely physical object. But at least we know that information about the weight of the object and its direction and velocity at a given point would be relevant to our prediction. So, too, we know something about the relevant factors in plotting the path of a precedent. We know that the line of motion of any precedent is subjected to a special pull that skews it whenever it passes near a point of high value tension. A series of precedents that shows a straight line when the judgments range from $1,000 to $100,000 may swerve pretty sharply when a case involves a twenty million dollar judgment against a government or other public institution that cannot make such a payment without serious public repercussions. Precedents that point to the protection of civil liberties may suddenly dwindle in times of public hysteria, but after the hysteria subsides they may resume their original force and direction. [*Cohen added the following footnote to the article*: The attitudes towards Mormonism that prevailed in the 1880's are attitudes that most of us can easily recognize as hysterical because we do not share them today. The Supreme Court decisions which upheld elimination of Mormons from public office, their disfranchisement, and the confiscation of Mormon Church property justified these punitive measures on the ground that certain teachings of Mormonism were a "nefarious . . . blot on our civilization . . . contrary to the spririt of Christianity." *Mormon Church v. United States,* 136 U.S. 1, 49 (1890). Under the impact of this attitude the Supreme Court maintained that religious freedom comprised only freedom of inner beliefs and did not extend to "practices" or "propaganda." *Reynolds v. United States,* 98 U.S. 145 (1878); *Davis v. Beason,* 133 U.S. 333 (1890). . . .]

## QUESTIONS

1. Cohen says, "According to the common view, it is logical to follow precedents but illogical to make precedents." What do the words "logical" and "illogical" mean according to the "common view"?
2. According to Cohen, "Whether the respects in which two cases are alike are important is a question not of logic but of values." Discuss this idea in relation to the cases studied in this chapter.
3. Read Judge Willard Bartlett's dissent in *MacPherson v. Buick Motor Co.*, excerpted on page 142. Do you think Willard Bartlett's "selectivity grid" is different from Cardozo's? (Recall that Cardozo wrote the majority opinion.)

### Clark v. Burns (1875)*

*In* Clark v. Burns, *the defendants owned the Cunard Steamship line. The plaintiff was a passenger on a ship sailing from Liverpool, England, to New York. He had usual first-class accommodations, sharing a state room with another passenger. It was customary (for safety reasons) for the defendants not to allow state room doors to be locked. The plaintiff knew about this custom since he had previously made three voyages on the Cunard line. Before going to sleep one night, the plaintiff put his watch*

* 118 Mass. 275 (1875).

*in his waistcoat pocket. He then hung the coat on a hook in his state room. The next morning the watch was missing. Clark notified the captain, but a search proved fruitless. Clark brought a lawsuit after the defendants' ticket agent refused to reimburse him for the value of the watch. Clark claimed the defendants were negligent and should be held liable, arguing by analogy from the common-law rule that would hold an innkeeper liable under similar circumstances. Clark lost at trial, but appealed to the Supreme Court of Massachusetts.*

CHIEF JUSTICE GRAY delivered the opinion of the court:

The liabilities of common carriers† and innkeepers, though similar, are distinct. No one is subject to both liabilities at the same time, and with regard to the same property. The liability of an innkeeper extends only to goods put in his charge as keeper of a public house, and does not attach to a carrier who has no house and is engaged only in the business of transportation. The defendants, as owners of steamboats carrying passengers and goods for hire, were not innkeepers. They would be subject to the liability of common carriers for the baggage of passengers in their custody, and might perhaps be so liable for a watch of the passenger locked up in his trunk with other baggage. But a watch, worn by a passenger on his person by day, and kept by him within reach for use at night, whether retained upon his person, or placed under his pillow, or in a pocket of his clothing hanging near him, is not so intrusted to their custody and control as to make them liable for it as common carriers.

## QUESTION

1. Compare the reasoning here with that of Judge O'Brien in *Adams v. New Jersey Steamboat Co.* on pages 46-47. Judge O'Brien concluded that a steamboat was a "floating inn." How are a passenger ship and an inn similar? How are they different? After reading the opinion in *Clark v. Burns*, do you agree with Judge O'Brien?

## *Hynes v. New York Central Railroad Co. (1921)*\*

*Hynes v. New York Central Railroad Co. involves a sixteen-year-old boy who was electrocuted as he was about to jump into the Harlem River (a public waterway) in New York City. He was going to dive off a plank nailed into the bulkhead at the end of*

---

† A *common carrier* is a person or company, serving the public, in the business of transporting people or property. The common carrier is required by law to carry all passengers and cargo as long as the specified fare is paid.

\* 231 N.Y. 229, 131 N.E. 898 (1921).

*a right of way owned by the railroad. (A* right of way *is the strip of land on which railroad companies construct their tracks. Here the term refers to the actual land. Outside the context of railroad use,* right of way *refers to the right of one person to cross another's land.) Along this right of way, the railroad had strung high-tension wires on poles and crossarms in order to run its trains. Swimmers had been using the plank beneath the wires as a diving board for at least five years without any protest from the railroad. But as Hynes stood poised to dive, a crossarm and wires fell from a pole and struck him. Hynes's mother sued the railroad, alleging that it had been negligent. She lost her case when lower courts held that her son had no right to be where he was when struck. Because he was a trespasser, the courts held that the railroad did not owe him a duty of care. (A* trespasser *is someone who intentionally enters another's property without any consent or privilege.) The case eventually came before the New York Court of Appeals. This excerpt from the opinion of Judge Cardozo deals with the problem of how the boy should be classified under the law and therefore what duty of care he was owed.*

JUDGE CARDOZO:

     . . . Thus far the courts have held that Hynes at the end of the springboard above the public waters was a trespasser on the defendant's land. They have thought it immaterial that the board itself was a trespass, an encroachment on the public ways. They have thought it of no significance that Hynes would have met the same fate if he had been below the board and not above it. The board, they have said, was annexed to the defendant's bulkhead. By force of such annexation, it was to be reckoned as a fixture,[†] and thus constructively, if not actually, an extension of the land. The defendant was under a duty to use reasonable care that bather swimming or standing in the water should not be electrocuted by wires falling from its right of way. But to bathers diving from the springboard, there was no duty, we are told, unless the injury was the product of mere willfulness or wantonness, no duty of active vigilance to safeguard the impending structure. Without wrong to them, cross arms might be left to rot; wires highly charged with electricity might sweep them from their stand, and bury them in the subjacent waters. In climbing on the board, they became trespassers and outlaws. The conclusion is defended with much subtlety of reasoning, with much insistence upon its inevitableness as a merely logical deduction. A majority of the court are unable to accept it as the conclusion of the law.

     We assume, without deciding, that the springboard was a fixture, a permanent improvement of the defendant's right of way. Much might be said in favor of another view. We do not press the inquiry, for we are persuaded

---

     † A *fixture* is personal property that is fixed to real estate (or, sometimes, a building) in such a way that it comes to be considered a permanent part of the land.

that the rights of bathers do not depend upon these nice distinctions. Liability would not be doubtful, we are told, had the boy been diving from a pole, if the pole had been vertical. The diver in such a situation would have been separated from the defendant's freehold [land]. Liability, it is said, has been escaped because the pole was horizontal. The plank when projected lengthwise was an extension of the soil. We are to concentrate our gaze on the private ownership of the board. We are to ignore the public ownership of the circumambient spaces of water and of air. Jumping from a boat or a barrel, the boy would have been a bather in the river. Jumping from the end of a springboard, he was no longer, it is said, a bather, but a trespasser on a right of way.

Rights and duties in systems of living law are not built upon such quicksands.

Bathers in the Harlem River on the day of this disaster were in the enjoyment of a public highway, entitled to reasonable protection against destruction by the defendant's wires. They did not cease to be bathers entitled to the same protection while they were diving from encroaching objects or engaging in the sports that are common among swimmers. Such acts were not equivalent to an abandonment of the highway, a departure from its proper uses, a withdrawal from the waters, and an entry upon land. A plane of private right had been interposed between the river and the air, but public ownership was unchanged in the space below it and above. The defendant does not deny that it would have owed a duty to this boy if he had been leaning against the springboard with his feet upon the ground. He is said to have forfeited protection as he put his feet upon the plank. Presumably the same result would follow if the plank had been a few inches above the surface of the water instead of a few feet. Duties are thus supposed to arise and to be extinguished in alternate zones or strata. Two boys walking in the country or swimming in a river stop to rest for a moment along the side of the road or the margin of the stream. One of them throws himself beneath the overhanging branches of a tree. The other perches himself on a bough a foot or so above the ground. . . . Both are killed by falling wires. The defendant would have us say that there is a remedy for the representatives of one, and none for the representatives of the other. We may be permitted to distrust the logic that leads to such conclusions. . . .

This case is a striking instance of the dangers of "a jurisprudence of conceptions" (Pound, Mechanical Jurisprudence, 8 Columbia Law Review, 605, 608, 610), the extension of a maxim or a definition with relentless disregard of consequences to "a dryly logical extreme." The approximate and relative become the definite and absolute. Landowners are not bound to regulate their conduct in contemplation of the presence of trespassers intruding upon private structures. Landowners are bound to regulate their conduct in contemplation of the presence of travelers upon the adjacent public ways. There are times when there is little trouble in marking off the field of exemption and immunity from that of liability and duty. Here structures and ways are so united and commingled, superimposed upon each other, that the fields are brought together. In such circumstances, there is little help in pursuing general maxims to ultimate conclusions. They have been framed *alio intuitu* [having another view or object]. They must be reformulated and readapted to meet exceptional conditions. Rules appropriate to spheres which are conceived of as separate and distinct cannot, both, be enforced when the spheres become concentric. There must then be readjustment or collision. In one sense, and that a highly technical and artificial one, the diver at the end of the springboard is an intruder on the adjoining lands. In another sense, and one that realists will accept more readily, he is still on public waters in the exercise of public rights. The law must say whether it will subject him to the rule of the one field or of the other, of this sphere or of that. We think that considerations of analogy, of convenience, of policy, and of justice, exclude him from the field of the defendant's immunity and exemption, and place him in the field of liability and duty.

## QUESTIONS

1. What are the classification questions in this case?
2. What is the point of Judge Cardozo's example about the two boys walking in the country or swimming in a river who are injured when they stop to rest?
3. Does this case set any precedent or stand for any broad rule of law? What is it?
4. Consider the following comment by Edwin J. Patterson:

   In the famous Hynes case a boy who had trespassed on railroad property adjoining a river and who was about to dive from a springboard affixed to that property and extending seven feet over public waters (the Harlem River) was struck and killed by the falling of the railroad company's defectively maintained electric wires. The lower courts, applying inexorably the rule that no duty of care is owed to the trespasser, had denied his mother's claim for damages. In the Court of Appeals Cardozo by persuasive rhetoric and ingenious casuistry changed the boy's situation from that of a trespasser on railroad property (the springboard) to that of a bather lawfully in public waters (the river below), thus convincing three of his colleagues that the defendant owed the boy a duty of care. What effect does the holding have on the rule, sometimes harsh in application, that a landowner need not keep his land in a safe condition for trespassers? Not that it is rejected or even modified; only that the Court will seek to exclude marginal cases from its operation.*

In the light of the *Hynes* case and this comment, do you think that legal classifications can be strictly drawn?

5. Do you find any similarities between the issues here and those in *Niederman v. Brodsky* in the materials for Chapter 2?
6. Examine the last sentence of Cardozo's opinion in *Hynes*. Cardozo mentions "considerations of analogy, of convenience, of policy and of justice." Which do you think carried the most weight in Cardozo's decision? Why?

## *MacPherson v. Buick Motor Co. (1916), Dissenting Opinion*†

*The* MacPherson *case was decided by a vote of 5 to 1, with Judge Cardozo writing the opinion of the court. Chief Judge Willard Bartlett was the sole dissenter. Here is an excerpt from his dissent.*

CHIEF JUDGE WILLARD BARTLETT, dissenting:

The case of Devlin v. Smith (89 N.Y. 470) is cited as an authority in conflict with the view that the liability of the manufacturer and vendor [seller] extends to third parties only when the article manufactured and sold is inherently dangerous. In that case the builder of a scaffold ninety feet high which was erected for the purpose of enabling painters to stand upon it, was held to be liable to the administratrix‡ of a painter who fell therefrom and was killed, being at the time in the employ of the person for whom the scaffold was built. It is said that the scaffold if properly constructed was not inherently dangerous; and hence that this decision affirms the existence of liability in the case of an article not dangerous in itself but made so only in consequence of negligent construction. Whatever logical force there may be in this view it seems to me clear from the language of Judge Rapallo, who wrote the opinion of the court, that the scaffold was deemed to be an inherently dangerous structure; and that the case was decided as it was because

---

* Edwin J. Patterson, *Jurisprudence* (Brooklyn, N.Y.: Foundation Press, 1953), pp. 534-35.
† 217 N.Y. 382, 395; 111 N.E. 1050, 1055 (1916).
‡ An administratrix *is a female who is appointed by a court to manage a deceased person's assets and liabilities. A male performing this task is called an* administrator. *If the decedent's will specifies a person to fill this role, the person is called an executor (male) or executrix (female).*

the court entertained that view. Otherwise he would hardly have said, as he did, that the circumstances seemed to bring the case fairly within the principle of Thomas v. Winchester.

I do not see how we can uphold the judgment in the present case without overruling what has been so often said by this court and other courts of like authority in reference to the absence of any liability for negligence on the part of the original vendor of an ordinary carriage to any one except his immediate vendee [buyer]. The absence of such liability was the very point actually decided in the English case of Winterbottom v. Wright, . . . and the illustration quoted from the opinion of Chief Judge Ruggles in Thomas v. Winchester . . . assumes that the law on the subject was so plain that the statement would be accepted almost as a matter of course. In the case at bar the defective wheel on an automobile moving only eight miles an hour was not any more dangerous to the occupants of the car than a similarly defective wheel would be to the occupants of a carriage drawn by a horse at the same speed; and yet, unless the courts have been all wrong on this question up to the present time, there would be no liability to strangers to the original sale in the case of the horse-drawn carriage.

## QUESTIONS

1. Is this a good criticism of Cardozo's reasoning in the case?
2. Is Willard Bartlett a better follower of precedent than Cardozo?
3. Is this dissenting opinion consistent with Judge Willard Bartlett's opinion in *Torgesen v. Schultz* in Chapter 3?

# Bibliographic Essay

Many users of this book will find it useful (and some may find it necessary) to read it in conjunction with an introductory text in logic. Such texts are legion. Among those that can be recommended are M. Copi, *Introduction to Logic*, 6th ed. (New York: Macmillan, 1982) and M. C. Beardsley, *Practical Logic* (New York: Prentice-Hall, 1950). See also, W. C. Salmon, *Logic*, 2nd ed. (Englewood Cliffs, N.J.: Prentice-Hall, 1973); F. R. Berger, *Studying Deductive Logic* (Englewood Cliffs, N.J.: Prentice-Hall, 1977).

Also useful as background is H. J. Abraham, *The Judicial Process*, 4th ed. (New York: Oxford University Press, 1980), which provides an extensive account of the structure and operations of appellate courts, and covers England and France as well as the United States. The book contains topically organized bibliographies. Of particular interest is Abraham's discussion of the power of the U. S. Supreme Court to declare legislative acts unconstitutional. Arthur T. Vanderbilt, *The Doctrine of Separation of Powers* (Lincoln, Neb.: University of Nebraska Press, 1953) is a useful general treatment of executive, legislative, and judicial powers.

The psychology of judicial decision making is still largely unexplored (and perhaps unexplorable) territory. For a judge's statement, see J. C. Hutcheson, "The Judgment Intuitive: The Function of the 'Hunch' in Judicial Decision," 14 *Cornell L. Q.* 274 (1929), which is referred to in the excerpt from Jerome Frank (included in the materials for Chapter 1). Frank purports to present a "Freudian" perspective on judicial decisions. Chapter 8 of E.G. Robinson, *Law and the Lawyers* (New York: Macmillan, 1935) also discusses judicial psychology. Perhaps the best way to get a "feel" for judicial psychology is by reading biographies of judges. G. E. White, *The American Judicial Tradition* (New York: Oxford University Press, 1976), which provides profiles of a number of leading American judges, has a bibliography that will direct students to the literature. Accessible and controversial portraits of Justices Holmes and Cardozo are presented in J. T. Noonan, *Persons and Masks of the Law* (New York: Farrar, Straus and Giroux, 1976). Judicial "behavior" has been extensively studied by political scientists through the use of statistical methods, in order to discern the effect on judicial voting patterns of such factors as party affiliation, appointing president, location of court, etc. A bibliography may be found in R.

A. Carp and C. K. Rowland, *Policymaking and Politics in the Federal District Courts* (Knoxville, Tenn.: University of Tennessee Press, 1983).

Numerous books and articles deal with the judicial process and judicial method. The term "judicial process" was popularized by Justice Benjamin N. Cardozo in his *The Nature of the Judicial Process* (New Haven: Yale University Press, 1921); this book is a classic. Topics treated under these rubrics often go beyond the scope of legal reasoning as it is considered in this textbook. General accounts of judicial process and method may be found in texts on jurisprudence by such authors as Allen, Bodenheimer, Dias, Friedmann, Lloyd of Hampstead, Paton, Patterson, and Salmond. S. Mermin, *Law and the Legal Process*, 2nd ed. (Boston: Little, Brown, 1982) supplies a good overview. *The Nature and Functions of Law*, 4th ed. (Mineola, N.Y.: Foundation Press, 1980), by H. J. Berman and W. R. Greiner, contains an extensive treatment of these and many other subjects; Chapters 5 and 6 use case illustrations from "manufacturer's liability in tort." Discussions of precedent in the above books usually consider the role of formal and analogical reasoning in court opinions; see also R. C. Cross, *Precedent in English Law*, 3rd ed. (Oxford: Clarendon Press, 1977).

Legal reasoning and the justification of judicial decisions are discussed in articles, by various hands, in the following books: C. Friedrich (ed.), *Rational Decision*, NOMOS VII (New York: Atherton Press, 1967); S. Hook (ed.), *Law and Philosophy* (New York: New York University Press, 1964); and G. Hughes, *Law, Reason, and Justice* (New York: New York University Press, 1969). An idealized model for legal reasoning is presented in G. Christie, "Objectivity in Legal Reasoning," 78 *Yale L.J.* 1311 (1969); see also Christie's book, *Law, Norms and Authority* (London: Duckworth, 1982). An analysis of models may also be found in P. Weiler, "Two Models of Judicial Decision Making," 46 *Canadian Bar Rev.* 406 (1968). John Dewey approaches the subject of judicial reasoning from the perspective of an "instrumental" logic in "Logical Method and Law," 10 *Cornell L. Q.* 17 (1924). R. Wasserstrom, *The Judicial Decision* (Stanford, Calif.: Stanford University Press, 1961), supports a two-level procedure, according to which a decision is justifiable if and only if it is deducible from a rule that can be shown to be more desirable than any other possible rule. Utilitarianism and legal justification are discussed in D. H. Hodgson, *Consequences of Utilitarianism: A Study in Normative Ethics and Legal Theory* (Oxford: Clarendon Press, 1967). Analogies between moral and judicial reasoning are illuminated in Thomas D. Perry, *Moral Reasoning and Truth* (Oxford: Clarendon Press, 1976).

One of the works on the "logic" of judicial reasoning most referred to is E. H. Levi, *Introduction to Legal Reasoning* (Chicago: University of Chicago Press, 1948), whose approach is described on page 103 of this book. A critique of Levi on reasoning by example is presented in C. Prevots, "On the Nature of Legal Deliberation," 49 *The Monist* 424 (1965). Levi's position is also discussed in J. Horovitz, *Law and Logic* (Wien and New York: Springer-Verlag, 1972), which also critically examines various theories of logic in legal reasoning put forth by continental and Anglo-American writers. Horovitz makes a brief for an "inductive legal logic." A short, general discussion on the role of logic is given by A. G. Guest, "Logic in the Law," in A. G. Guest (ed.), *Oxford Essays in Jurisprudence* (Oxford: Clarendon Press, 1961). Relevant literature is also contained in edited collections of readings in jurisprudence (e.g., by Cohen and Cohen, Hall, and Christie).

On the place of formal logic and deductive arguments in the law, see D. N. Mac-Cormick, "Formal Justice and the Form of Legal Arguments," 19 *Logique et Analyse* 108 (1976), and the same author's book, *Legal Reasoning and Legal Theory* (Oxford: Clarendon Press, 1978), Chapters 2 and 3. Numerous articles in English on this topic can be found in the journals *Logique et Analyse* and *Archiv fur Rechts-und Sozialphilosophie*, but a good grounding in symbolic logic is necessary in order to follow many of them. (Caution, however, must be exercised in reading literature of this type; the quality tends to be uneven.) A much debated issue in these journals is whether or not legal reasoning has a logic of "its own"; see also the book by Horovitz, cited above. Symbolic logic is employed by I. Tammelo, *Modern Logic in the Service of Law* (Wien and New York: Springer-Verlag, 1978); the author adds, however, that deductive logic does not exhaust all forms of legal reasoning. The role and limits of logic in law are discussed in Chapters 6, 7, and 8 of J. Stone, *Legal System and Lawyers' Reasonings* (Stanford: Stanford University Press, 1964); a critical discussion of Stone is contained in Horovitz's book. Ch. Perelman also argues that formal logic is of limited use in his *Justice, Law, and Argument* (Dordrecht, Holland: D. Riedel, 1980). He presents an alternative approach, based on Aristotle's *Topics* and *Rhetoric*, for political and moral as well as legal argumentation; see Ch. Perelman and L. Olbrechts-Tyteca, *The New Rhetoric* (Notre Dame: University of Notre Dame Press, 1969). Perelman's views are criticized in K. Sinclair, "Legal Reasoning: In Search of an Adequate Theory of Argument," 59 *California L.R.* 821 (1971), which contains a survey of some of the literature on the topic; this article also employs symbolic logic. Deontic logic (which studies the logical relations of such notions as permission and obligation) has been used to investigate the structure of legal concepts and legal systems, but most of the works in this area are highly technical. Two books that bear on problems in legal philosophy, and which are not excessively formal, are: A. Ross, *Directives and Norms* (London: Routledge and Kegan Paul, 1968); G. H. von Wright, *Norm and Action* (New York: Humanities Press, 1963), Chapters 1, 5, 6, 7, and 10.

On the idea of principled decision, see M. P. Golding, "Principled Judicial Decision-Making," 73 *Ethics* 247 (1963), and M. P. Golding, "Principled Decision-making and the Supreme Court," 63 *Columbia L.R.* 35 (1963). The latter article discusses the important paper by H. Wechsler, "Towards Neutral Principles of Constitutional Law," 73 *Harvard L.R.* 1 (1959). The subject is brought up-to-date in K. Greenawalt, "The Enduring Search for Neutral Principles," 78 *Columbia L.R.* 982 (1978).

The view that judges sometimes exercise a legislative, lawmaking role is presented in Justice Oliver W. Holmes's classic article "The Path of the Law," 10 *Harvard L.R.* 457 (1897). J. C. Gray, *The Nature and Sources of the Law*, 2nd ed. (New York: Macmillan, 1921), also a classic of American jurisprudence, argues that the courts are the true lawmakers. M. R. Cohen, who nevertheless held that there is a workable distinction between judicial adherence to rule and the exercise of discretion, criticizes that "phonograph theory" of judicial decision making in the "The Process of Judicial Legislation," in his *Law and the Social Order,* reprint (New Brunswick, N.J.: Transaction Books, 1982).

Much of the recent discussion of the extent to which judges are free to exercise their own discretion takes its departure from H. L. A. Hart, *The Concept of Law* (Oxford: Clarendon Press, 1961), Chapter 7. Hart rejects both "formalism" (judges are nevèr free, because the proper decision is logically determined by pre-existent law) and "rule-skepticism" (judges are never "bound" to decide cases as they do). A very useful article on the subject is K. Greenawalt "Discretion and Judicial Decision: The Elusive Quest for the Fetters that Bind " 75 *Columbia L.R.* 359 (1975). Greenawalt includes a critical discussion of the views of R. Sartorius and R. M. Dworkin, who criticize each other but arrive at a somewhat similar conclusion (reminiscent of, but not identical with, "formalism"). See Sartorius, "The Justification of the Judicial Decision," 78 *Ethics* 171 (1968); Sartorius, "Social Policy and Judicial Legislation," 8 *Amer. Philosophical Quart.* 151 (1971); Sartorius, *Individual Conduct and Social Norms* (Encino, Calif.: Dickenson, 1975), Chapter 10; Dworkin, *Taking Rights Seriously,* expanded ed. (Cambridge, Mass.: Harvard University Press, 1978), Chapters 2, 3, 4, and 13; Dworkin, "No Right Answer?," 53 *N.Y.U.L.R.* 1 (1978). Hart is severly criticized by Dworkin in Chapters 2 and 3 of *Taking Rights Seriously.* Dworkin is notorious for holding that there is a uniquely "right answer," which judges are duty-bound to give, for each question of law, even though the grounds of the decision are "inherently controversial." Discussion of Dworkin amounts to a minor industry. For a brief and incisive critique see H. L. A. Hart, "American Jurisprudence Through English Eyes: The Nightmare and the Noble Dream," 11 *Georgia L.R.* 969 (1977). Almost an entire issue (no. 5) of 11 *Georgia L.R.* (1977) is devoted to Dworkin, who gives a response, "Seven Critics," that is reprinted in *Taking Rights Seriously.* Another example of criticism is A. D. Woozley, "No Right Answer," 29 *Philosophical Quart.* 25 (1979).

On legal philosophy, see H. L. A. Hart, "Philosophy of Law, Problems of," *The Encyclopedia of Philosophy* (New York: Collier-Macmillan, 1967), vol. 6, 264–276; M. P. Golding, *Philosophy of Law* (Englewood Cliffs, N.J.: Prentice-Hall, 1975); R. Pound, *An Introduction to the Philosophy of Law* (New Haven: Yale University Press, 1922). The classic work in English of the second half of the twentieth century is H. L. A. Hart's *The Concept of Law,* cited above. Selections from Hart and other writers on the definition of "law" may be found in M. P. Golding (ed.), *The Nature of Law* (New York: Random House, 1966). Selections from various writers on this and other topics in legal philosophy may be found in anthologies edited by E. Kent and by J. Feinberg and H. Gross. R. W. M. Dias, *A Bibliography of Jurisprudence,* 3rd ed. (London: Butterworths, 1979), is arranged topically and will provide leads for further study.

# Index

*Abernethy v. Hutchinson* (1825), 80
Abinger, Lord, 24, 25, 27, 30, 33, 101, 113
acceptability:
  as criterion of good reasons, 9, 10, 56
  reasoning as attempt to establish, 6
  strength of argument and, 2–3
  *See also* truth
action, cause of, in *Lubitz v. Wells*, 36
action, right of, in *Dietrich v. Inhabitants of Northampton*, 91, 92
action *per quod servitium amisit,* defined, 76*n*
*Adams v. New Jersey Steamboat Co.* (1896), 46–49, 102–106, 108–110, 138
administratrix, defined, 142*n*
adversary method, 7, 8
*Aero Spark Plug Co. v. B. G. Co.,* 131
analogical arguments, 42, 44–49
  in *Adams v. New Jersey Steamboat Co.,* 46–49, 102–106, 108–110, 138
  conclusions of, 45, 46, 48, 107–111, 114
  interpretations and revisions of, 102–111
"appeal to justice and fairness" kind of reason
  in *Riggs v. Palmer,* 84–85
  in *Summers v. Tice,* 75
"appeal to the law" kind of reason, 53
appeal to precedents, 95
  kinds of, 101
  *See also* precedents
"appeal to public policy" kind of reason, 47–48, 60*n*, 85
  *See also* goal-oriented reasons
arbitrariness:
  adherence to precedents eliminating, 99

149

## About the Author

Martin P. Golding is professor of philosophy and law at Duke University, where he also serves as chairman of the department of philosophy. He is a graduate of the University of California at Los Angeles and received his Ph.D. from Columbia University. He previously taught at Columbia and at the John Jay College of Criminal Justice, in New York, and has taught as a visitor at a number of universities. Since 1969, Professor Golding has served as the secretary-treasurer of the American Society for Political and Legal Philosophy. He is the editor of *The Nature of Law* (1966) and the author of *Philosophy of Law* (1975). He has also published articles on legal philosophy, moral philosophy, and bioethics.

## A Note on the Type

The text of this book was set in a computer version of Times Roman, designed by Stanley Morison for *The Times* (London) and first introduced by that newspaper in 1932.

Among typographers and designers of the twentieth century, Stanley Morison has been a strong forming influence as typographical adviser to the English Monotype Corporation, as a director of two distinguished English publishing houses, and as a writer of sensibility, erudition, and keen practical sense.

Typography by Barbara Sturman. Cover design by Maria Epes. Composition by Publishers Extension, Inc., Ann Arbor, Michigan Printed and bound by Banta Company, Menasha, Wisconsin.

# BORZOI BOOKS
# IN LAW AND AMERICAN SOCIETY

## Law and American History

### EARLY AMERICAN LAW AND SOCIETY
Stephen Botein, *Michigan State University*

This volume consists of an essay dealing with the nature of law and early American socioeconomic development from the first settlements to 1776. The author shows how many legal traditions sprang both from English experience and from the influence of the New World. He explores the development of transatlantic legal structures in order to show how they helped rationalize intercolonial affairs. Mr. Botein also emphasizes the relationship between law and religion. The volume includes a pertinent group of documents for classroom discussion, and a bibliographic essay.

### LAW IN THE NEW REPUBLIC: *Private Law and the Public Estate*
George Dargo, *Brookline, Massachusetts*

Though the American Revolution had an immediate and abiding impact on American public law (e.g., the formation of the federal and state constitutions), its effect on private law (e.g., the law of contracts, tort law) was less direct but of equal importance. Through essay and documents, Mr. Dargo examines post-Revolutionary public and private reform impulses and finds a shifting emphasis from public to private law which he terms "privatization." To further illustrate the tension between public and private law, the author develops a case study (the Batture land controversy in New Orleans) in early nineteenth century legal, economic, and political history. The volume includes a wide selection of documents and a bibliographic essay.

### LAW IN ANTEBELLUM SOCIETY: *Legal Change and Economic Expansion*
Jamil Zainaldin, *Washington, D.C.*

This book examines legal change and economic expansion in the first half of the nineteenth century, integrating major themes in the development of law with key historical themes. Through a series of topical essays and the use of primary source materials, it describes how political, social, and economic interests and values influence law making. The book's focus is on legislation and the common law.

### LAW AND THE NATION, 1865–1912
Jonathan Lurie, *Rutgers University*

Using the Fourteenth Amendment as the starting point for his essay, Mr. Lurie examines the ramifications of this landmark constitutional provision on the economic and social development of America in the years following the Civil War. He also explores important late nineteenth-century developments in legal education, and concludes his narrative with some insights on law and social change in the first decade of the twentieth century. The volume is highlighted by a documents section containing statutes, judicial opinions, and legal briefs, with appropriate questions for classroom discussion. Mr. Lurie's bibliographic essay provides information to stimulate further investigation of this period.

ORDERED LIBERTY: *Legal Reform in the Twentieth Century*
Gerald L. Fetner, *University of Chicago*

In an interpretive essay, the author examines the relationship between several major twentieth-century reform movements (e.g., Progressivism, New Deal, and the Great Society) and the law. He shows how policy makers turned increasingly to the legal community for assistance in accommodating economic and social conflict, and how the legal profession responded by formulating statutes, administrative agencies, and private arrangements. Mr. Fetner also discusses how the organization and character of the legal profession were affected by these social changes. Excerpts from relevant documents illustrate issues discussed in the essay. A bibliographic essay is included.

## Law and Philosophy

### DISCRIMINATION AND REVERSE DISCRIMINATION
Kent Greenawalt, *Columbia Law School*

Using discrimination and reverse discrimination as a model, Mr. Greenawalt examines the relationship between law and ethics. He finds that the proper role of law cannot be limited to grand theory concerning individual liberty and social restraint, but must address what law can effectively discover and accomplish. Such concepts as distributive and compensatory justice and utility are examined in the context of preferential treatment for blacks and other minorities. The analysis draws heavily on the Supreme Court's Bakke decision. The essay is followed by related documents, primarily judicial opinions, with notes and questions, and a bibliography.

### THE LEGAL ENFORCEMENT OF MORALITY
Thomas Grey, *Stanford Law School*

This book deals with the traditional issue of whether morality can be legislated and enforced. It consists of an introductory essay and legal texts on three issues: the enforcement of sexual morality, the treatment of human remains, and the duties of potential rescuers. The author shows how philosophical problems differ from classroom hypotheticals when they are confronted in a legal setting. He illustrates this point using material from statutes, regulations, judicial opinions, and law review commentaries. Mr. Grey reviews the celebrated Hart-Devlin debate over the legitimacy of prohibiting homosexual acts. He places the challenging problem of how to treat dead bodies, arising out of developments in the technology of organ transplantation, in the context of the debate over morals enforcement, and discusses the Good Samaritan as an issue concerning the propriety of the legal enforcement of moral duties.

### LEGAL REASONING
Martin Golding, *Duke University*

This volume is a blend of text and readings. The author explores the many sides to legal reasoning—as a study in judicial psychology and, in a more narrow sense, as an inquiry into the "logic" of judicial decision making. He shows how judges justify their rulings, and gives examples of the kinds of arguments they use. He challenges the notion that judicial reasoning is rationalization; instead, he argues that judges are guided by a deep concern for consistency and by a strong need to have their decisions stand as a measure for the future conduct of individuals. *(Forthcoming in 1984)*

# LAW AND AMERICAN LITERATURE
*A one-volume collection of the following three essays:*

## Law as Form and Theme in American Letters
### Carl S. Smith, *Northwestern University*

The author explores the interrelationships between law aned literature generally and be-tween American law and American literature in particular. He explores first the literary qualities of legal writing and then the attitudes of major American writers toward the law. Throughout, he studies the links between the legal and literary imaginations. He finds that legal writing has many literary qualities that are essential to its function, and he points out that American writers have long been wary of the power of the law and its special language, speaking out as a compensating voice for the ideal of justice.

## Innocent Criminal or Criminal Innocence: The Trial in American Fiction
### John McWilliams, *Middlebury College*

Mr. McWilliams explores how law functions as a standard for conduct in a number of major works of American literature, including Cooper's *The Pioneers,* Melville's *Billy Budd,* Dreiser's *An American Tragedy,* and Wright's *Native Son.* Each of these books ends in a criminal trial, in which the reader is asked to choose between his emotional sympathy for the victim and his rational understanding of society's need for criminal sanctions. The author compares these books with James Gould Cozzens' *The Just and the Unjust,* a study of a small town legal system, in which the people's sense of justice contravenes traditional authority.

## Law and Lawyers in American Popular Culture
### Maxwell Bloomfield, *Catholic University of America*

Melding law, literature, and the American historical experience into a single essay, Mr. Bloomfield discusses popular images of the lawyer. The author shows how contempo-rary values and attitudes toward the law are reflected in fiction. He concentrates on two historical periods: antebellum America and the Progressive era. He examines fictional works which were not always literary classics, but which exposed particular legal mores. An example of such a book is Winston Churchill's *A Far Country* (1915), a story of a successful corporation lawyer who abandons his practice to dedicate his life to what he believes are more socially desirable objectives.